John Grider's Century

African Americans in Solano, Napa, and Sonoma Counties from 1845 to 1925

Sharon McGriff-Payne

Dr. Taylor:
Thank you for
continuing to tell our
wonderful story.
Sharon McGriff-Payne
10-29-09

iUniverse, Inc.
New York   Bloomington

John Grider's Century
African Americans in Solano, Napa, and Sonoma Counties from 1845 to 1925

Copyright © 2009 Sharon McGriff-Payne

iUniverse books may be ordered through booksellers or by contacting:

iUniverse
1663 Liberty Drive
Bloomington, IN 47403
www.iuniverse.com
1-800-Authors (1-800-288-4677)

ISBN: 978-1-4401-6091-2 (pbk)
ISBN: 978-1-4401-6093-6 (cloth)
ISBN: 978-1-4401-6092-9 (ebk)

Printed in the United States of America

iUniverse rev. date: 9/10/2009

To my parents, Marshall and Bernice McGriff,
who helped blaze new trails for me.

We must go beyond textbooks, go out into the bypaths
and untrodden depths of the wilderness and travel and
explore and tell the world the glories of our journey.
—John Hope Franklin

Contents

Acknowledgments

Many hands have gone into the making of this book; so many people must be thanked. I owe so much to those early African American pioneers who, against all odds, made their way to the San Francisco North Bay in the nineteenth century. I offer this book as a small down payment on the enormous debt I owe these early pioneers.

I am also indebted to Delilah L. Beasley, author of *The Negro Trail Blazers of California*, who, a century ago, embarked on a mission to document the history of African Americans in the state. It is from the pages of her book that I learned of several black pioneers in our region. Thanks to the foresight of this remarkable woman, much of our rich history is known.

My sincerest thanks must go to my husband, Clarence Payne, who has been enormously patient and supportive throughout this project, and to Mel Orpilla and Belle Santos Orpilla, my former neighbors, who encouraged the research leading to this book. Sincere thanks go also to Guy Washington, Pacific West-Intermountain program manager for the National Park Service Network to Freedom Project. Guy reminded me of Delilah L.

Beasley's book and her references to the San Francisco North Bay African American pioneers. Guy, you are a great resource.

I will be forever thankful to the late Madeline Ontis of the city of Napa. In 2006, Mrs. Ontis sent me an early photograph of Julia Canner and her granddaughter Mazie Strickland that was taken around the early 1900s.

My heartfelt thanks go also to Leslie Batson and Ruth Setterquist at the Solano County Archives. Much of our shared history is housed at the Solano County Archives. The archives are truly one of our county's best-kept secrets; I hope it will eventually get the attention it deserves.

Special thanks to Jim Kern, executive director of the Vallejo Naval and Historical Museum, who proved so helpful in my research. I spent many afternoons in the deepest recesses of the museum where I learned a great deal about my hometown and its people. Katherine J. Rinehart, a library associate with the History and Genealogy Annex of the Sonoma County Library provided information on the African American pioneers who called Sonoma County home in the 1800s. Thanks, Katherine.

Thanks to Phil Reader, an independent researcher—from him I learned a great deal about Joseph McAfee, another African American Bear Flag Revolt veteran who, after the 1846 skirmish, lived in Benicia for a number of years.

I am especially grateful to the Prince Hall Grand Lodge of California for their excellent history that dates back to 1852. The Grand Lodge has kept impeccable records. African American men, who were at the forefront of the state's earliest civil rights movement in the nineteenth century, were often leaders of the state's earliest Masonic lodges. Thanks to these early records, I learned of the North Bay region's Masonic connections, which were extensive during the 1800s. Special thanks to Prince Hall Grand Historian Herby Price Jr. and Willie D. Humphrey, assistant grand historian, for their knowledge and assistance.

Special thanks must also go to Dolores Owens Cofer, Patricia Ledoux Johnson, and Catherine Fulcher for sharing photos and memories of their relatives who were among the earliest members of Vallejo's Firma Lodge No. 27. Dolores' father James Owens and Catherine Fulcher's great uncle, George W. Posey, were Buffalo Soldiers and were founding members of the Vallejo Masons, the NAACP, and the Second Baptist and Kyles Temple AME churches.

Thank you Donald Stamps, whose parents were in pre-World War I Vallejo. He helped me with information on Second Baptist Church, which he attended as a child in the 1930s. Mr. Stamps, a history buff in his own right, years ago compiled a list of African Americans who lived in Vallejo from around 1913. This list proved valuable for my research on Vallejo during the early twentieth century. Also thanks to James Williams who told me of the early Buffalo Soldiers and black clerks who worked at Mare Island during the early 1900s.

Thanks, too, to my brother Michael McGriff for letting me know when I got off course. "Just finish the book," Michael would tell me at least once a week during the last year of my research. Thank you, Morris and Phyllis Turner for reading my first drafts and being consistent and so well versed in African American history.

Especially helpful was my cousin Helen R. Peterson, who devoted so much time and effort to this project. Helen, who is an excellent writer, was thoughtful and skillful in assisting me with the small details of this project. Thanks to Daryl Bell for looking at my early drafts—even during some of your own challenging times, you were there. Thank you, Maria Guevara for your typing assistance and Jackie Nelson for your media support including the book cover design. I owe a great deal of gratitude to my friend Mary A. Miller, who listened to me recount the stories of these early pioneers. Mary, your enthusiasm and appreciation of this history kept me encouraged.

In closing, I am most grateful to my parents, Marshall and Bernice McGriff, who were pioneers in their own right when they left Lake Wales, Florida, in the early 1940s to make their way to

California, where my father, a sailor, was stationed at Mare Island. After a short return to Florida, my parents made their way back to Vallejo in 1951 with five children and a trailer in tow. In the spirit of those early black pioneers who came one hundred years before, Mom and Dad, you helped blaze a new trail for your children.

Ever grateful,
Sharon McGriff-Payne

Illustrations

Preface

I have lived in the North San Francisco Bay area of California for over fifty years—nearly all my life. And for a majority of that time, I was under the common impression that few, if any, African Americans called the North Bay area home during the nineteenth century. In compiling *John Grider's Century: African Americans in Solano, Napa, and Sonoma Counties from 1845–1925*, I have sought to put this myth to rest as much as possible.

My mother and father, Bernice and Marshall McGriff, came to Vallejo, California, during the great migration of the 1940s, which brought many African Americans from the South to work in West Coast shipyards. I was raised in Vallejo, and I took for granted our city's strong racial diversity. I always shared classrooms with white, black, Asian, and Hispanic classmates. I thought I knew the North Bay region well, but what I knew about Vallejo's early black community could fit in the palm of my hand with room to spare. I was aware that during the early 1900s Vallejo's black community formally organized two houses of worship, the Second Baptist Church and Kyles Temple African Methodist Episcopal Zion Church, which continue to provide spiritual guidance to this day. I also knew that Vallejo's National

Association for the Advancement of Colored People (NAACP) was one of California's earliest branches, chartered in 1918. I was also aware that Prince Hall Masons, Firma Lodge No. 27, was organized around the same time. That was the extent of my knowledge of the North Bay's early black community.

In the 1970s, while a student at Sonoma State College (now Sonoma State University) in Rohnert Park, I embraced that time-period and its emphasis on African American history and culture. It was because of that love that I discovered *The Negro Trail Blazers of California* by Delilah L. Beasley in the school library. I was in awe of Beasley, who set out in 1908 to document the history of California's black pioneers. From Beasley's book, I learned of longtime Vallejo resident John Grider, an African American veteran of the 1846 Bear Flag Revolt at Sonoma, an event that helped set the stage for California statehood. I was surprised to read about Grider and the other North Bay African Americans Beasley listed. Though I had attended public school in Vallejo from kindergarten through high school and learned California history, John Grider was not mentioned once. I had never made the connection between Vallejo's rich ethnic mix and our region's deep maritime roots.

In 2006, while researching the North Bay's connection to the Underground Railroad for a freelance piece I was writing, John Grider's name resurfaced. I reread Beasley's book. My curiosity was aroused, and I began to explore the history in more depth. Imagine my surprise when, in my research and through talking to longtime residents of the area, I discovered that people of African descent were here well before California's statehood.

This book grew out of pure curiosity and a desire to "pay back" all those African American men and women who encouraged me as I grew up. I realized that I could not write their individual stories, so this book is my way of honoring their memory. The idea of writing about African American history had started to percolate in my mind partly because my former neighbors Mel and Belle Orpilla had encouraged me to do so. Mel had written a book about Filipinos in Vallejo and thought I should write about our city's early black history.

As I researched this book, I learned that our region's early shipping industry, bolstered by Mare Island Naval Shipyard, contributed greatly to our region's rich ethnic mix. From our region's birth nearly 160 years ago, people came from all over the world—China, the United Kingdom, the West Indies, Africa, and all parts of the United States—to make our region what it is today.

I had been trapped by my own distorted belief that so few black people lived in the North Bay that no one had bothered to keep their records. While writing this book, however, I realized how many more stories about the North Bay's African American community remain to be told. By documenting this history, we will continue to move closer to knowing the real North Bay story. My greatest hope is that readers will recognize an ancestor. I believe there are many descendants still in the North Bay, and perhaps this book will help those who are searching for more information on their families.

Timeline of North Bay Area African Americans (1826–1925)

This timeline reflects the nearly eight decades John Grider spent in the North Bay and the progress made by African Americans, locally and nationwide, over the course of those eight decades.

April 17, 1826 - John Grider is born into slavery in Tennessee.

1845 - John Grider, his owner George Wyatt, and other men cross the plains for California.

June 14, 1846 - The Bear Flag Revolt at Sonoma.

1848 - Gold is struck at Sutter's Fort.

1849 - The California Constitutional Convention is held in Monterey. Among a host of extremely discriminatory legislation, delegates vote to disenfranchise "Indians, Africans, and decedents of Africans."

1850 - California admitted into the Union on September 9 as a "free state." Solano County is made one of the state's original 27 counties. The Solano County census reports that of the twenty-one black men and women enumerated in the county, fourteen are slaves under contract in Vacaville to work for two years, after which they will be set free.

1851–1853 - Vallejo serves as California's capitol.

1852 - State legislators in Vallejo pass California's version of the Fugitive Slave Act.

1854 - Mare Island Navy Yard is established.

September 17, 1855 - After paying $1 to his owner Singleton Vaughn, Adam Willis is manumitted, or set free, by a Benicia court judge.

November 20-22, 1855 - The first Convention of the Colored Citizens of the State of California is held in Sacramento.

Dec. 9-12, 1856 - The second Convention of the Colored Citizens of the State of California is held in Sacramento

Oct.13-16, 1857 - The third Convention of the Colored Citizens of the State of California meets in San Francisco.

August 10, 1860 - L. J. Williams, a future leader of Vallejo's African American community during the early- to mid-twentieth century, is born into slavery in Chillicothe, Missouri.

1861 - Civil War declared.

January 1, 1863 - President Lincoln signs the Emancipation Proclamation, freeing—at least on paper—millions of American slaves. Celebrations are held throughout the Bay Area and North Bay.

January 14, 1863 - Grand Jubilee celebration marking the Emancipation Proclamation is held at Platts Music Hall in San Francisco.

August 1863 - John Grider and scores of other Solano County men sign up for the mandatory Union Draft. Grider, age thirty-seven, is listed as twenty-eight.

1864 - Union (African) Methodist Episcopal Church is established in Petaluma.

April 9, 1865 - General Robert E. Lee surrenders to General Ulysses S. Grant at Appomattox Court House in Virginia, ending the Civil War.

April 14, 1865 - President Abraham Lincoln assassinated; days later Vallejo resident Edward Hatton proposes that all black people contribute $1 to go toward a fund to build a mansion for his widow, Mary Todd Lincoln. A portion of the funds raised would also help build a cottage for John Brown's widow.

June 6, 1865 - Elizabeth Bundy, a cook, buys a home for $800 on D Street in Benicia. Her purchase makes her one of the first African American women to buy property in Solano County.

Oct. 25-28, 1865 - The fourth Convention of the Colored Citizens of the State of California is held in Sacramento.

1866 - After campaigning for better schools, African Americans, by state law, gain access to California public schools.

May 1867 - Napa's African Americans organize the African Methodist Episcopal Church on Washington Street in Napa. It is among the state's earliest AME churches.

December 21, 1867 - The play "Uncle Tom's Cabin" opened in Vallejo. Based on Harriet Beecher Stowe's anti-slavery novel, the play "was well played considering the short time in preparation" and bad weather. The actors included the Wilson Troupe and the Pixley Sisters.

January 1, 1870 - Hundreds, including many North Bay residents, attend the seventh anniversary celebration of the Emancipation Proclamation in San Francisco.

March 30, 1870 – The Fifteenth Amendment is ratified. African American men are granted the right to vote, and Frederick A. Sparrow, a Napa barber, is one of the first African Americans to register to vote in the North Bay.

April 11, 1870 - Celebrations to mark the Fifteenth Amendment's passage are held throughout the North Bay and Bay Area. A well-attended event is held in Napa where a 100-gun salute, speeches, and a dance marked the occasion.

April 22, 1872 - A statewide educational committee of African American men meet at Bethel AME Church in San Francisco to discuss the educational rights of African American students.

1874 - Vallejo school trustees vote to abolish the town's "colored school," and African American students are permitted to enroll in the general public school. Vallejo is among the earliest school districts to desegregate.

May 23, 1876 - Joseph McAfee, a Bear Flag veteran and former Benicia resident, dies in Santa Cruz at the age of fifty-seven.

1876 - Grider registers to vote for the first time.

1896 - The United States Supreme Court rules in the landmark *Plessy vs. Ferguson* case that "separate but equal" accommodations by state government are constitutional under the Equal Protection Clause.

1898 - The Spanish-American War takes place in April through August.

November 20, 1902 - Former Benicia slave Adam Willis, a "pioneer of pioneers," dies in Fairfield at the age of seventy-six.

1902-1903 - Joseph S. Hatton is named Most Worshipful Grand Master of the Prince Hall California Grand Lodge of Free and Accepted Masons.

Jan. 4, 1904 - Mary Ellen Pleasant, the San Francisco businesswoman who helped finance John Brown's raid at Harper's Ferry, dies.

May 17, 1904 - Robert Crooks, a survivor of the 1847 Donner Party incident, dies in Sonoma. Crooks was a longtime resident of Sonoma County.

November 28, 1905 - John Henry Turpin, a Navy mess attendant who survived explosions aboard the Battleship *Maine* (1898) and the USS *Bennington* (June 1905), takes on Matt Turner, another black boxer, in a boxing match at Vallejo's Palm Club.

September 14, 1907 - Vallejo's Second Baptist Church is founded in the home of J. L. and Sophia Malone.

1909 - Ellsworth Courtney of Vallejo becomes one of the first African American children to graduate from Vallejo High School, then located at Lincoln School.

1910 - Kyles Temple AME Zion Church is founded.

July 1910 - Vallejo's African American community celebrates boxer Jack Johnson's victory over Jim Jeffries held on the Fourth of July in Reno.

1911- Charles H. Toney, a Mare Island clerk, establishes the Vallejo Industrial and Normal Institute for colored children on Marin Street in Vallejo.

1913 - Grand United Order of Odd Fellows, El Dorado Lodge No. 9429, is organized in Vallejo.

July 28, 1914 - World War I begins.

September 9–10, 1914 - John Grider is among those feted in a huge Admission Day parade sponsored by the Native Sons of the Golden West in downtown Vallejo.

1915 - The first wave of the Great Migration begins, bringing millions of African Americans out of the South. Many of these southerners move to the North Bay seeking better pay, housing, and relief from the unrelenting racism of the South.

January 14, 1915 - Household of Ruth No. 458, the women's auxiliary to the Grand United Order of Odd Fellows, is organized in Vallejo. Officers include Lucy Crabb, Henrietta Bridges, Cellecta Jones, and Elizabeth Brown.

July 1917 - The Spanish American Veterans Hall at 1209 Georgia Street is completed and deeded.

June 22, 1917 - Sam Langford, dubbed "The Boston Terror," is scheduled to fight Jim West at Vallejo's Flosden Club.

August 11, 1917 - The Vallejo Colored Athletes, considered one of the premiere African American baseball teams in Northern California, plays in a Red Cross benefit game.

June 5, 1918 - Prince Hall Masons, Firma Lodge No. 27, is organized in Vallejo.

June 18, 1918 - The national office of the National Association for the Advancement of Colored People in New York officially endorses the NAACP branch in Vallejo.

November 11, 1918 - Armistice Day - ceasefire is declared in World War I.

November 28, 1919 - Kyles Temple AME Zion Church burns to the ground, the result of arsonists.

June 28, 1919 - The Treaty of Versailles is signed.

June 13, 1920 - Members of Firma Lodge No. 27 lay the cornerstone for Kyles Temple AME Zion Church at Illinois and Sonoma streets in Vallejo.

August 12, 1920 - Vallejo's NAACP establishes the Women's Political Club, six days before the Nineteenth Amendment, which gave women the right to vote, was ratified by Congress.

February 12–13, 1921 - Vallejo's NAACP hosts the Pacific Coast Conference at Lincoln School. In a fitting gesture, the conference begins on the "Great Emancipator's" birthday.

1923 - Fidelus Chapter No. 19, Order of Eastern Star, is organized in Vallejo.

December 22, 1924 - John Grider, believed to be one of the last known survivors of the Bear Flag Revolt, dies at the Fairfield County Hospital.

Delilah L. Beasley:
The Memory Keeper

Delilah L. Beasley

In the groundbreaking *The Negro Trail Blazers of California,* published ninety years ago, Delilah L. Beasley did what no other author had done before: she told the story of countless African Americans who helped shape the nation's thirty-first state. In her quest, Beasley came face-to-face with people who—just generations before—had crossed the plains and mined for gold, had known bondage, and had lived to see a new day and a new century. I wanted not only to know their stories but also to catch a glimpse into the life of Beasley, a woman who went "wherever a railroad or a horse and buggy could go."[1]

Beasley, a native of Springfield, Ohio, was a trailblazer in her own right when she moved west in 1908 to pursue her dream of writing the history of African American pioneers in California. With limited formal education and very little money, Beasley defied the prevailing sexism and racism of that era. During a period when women—white and black—married and stayed at home, Beasley moved across the country to document and tell the story of these early African American California pioneers. Her journey took her to public and private libraries where she met with leading educators of the day. She met with editors of newspapers, and she mined the memories of pioneers. What must they have thought of this fortyish black woman who dared to be so different?

By reading Beasley's work, I developed my own skills regarding research. She combed through old newspapers, letters, photo albums, and "poor farm" records. And save for researching poor farm records, so did I. She wrote every county board of supervisor's office in California seeking information on property and land records. Save for Marysville and Los Angeles, most county officials either did not reply or dismissed her inquiry saying they "knew nothing about the Negroes in that county." If Beasley was ever discouraged in her long search to tell early African American history in the golden state, her work didn't show it. Perseverance was a large part of the lesson I learned from Beasley.

---

1   Unless otherwise noted, all quotations from this chapter are from *The Negro Trail Blazers of California* by Delilah Beasley (1919).

Beasley notes that, because she was often in ill health, *The Negro Trail Blazers of California* took her "eight years and six months to the very day it was ready for the publisher." But thanks to Beasley's early research that began in 1908 and culminated with the 1919 publication of her book, much is now known about those African Americans, including many in the North Bay Area, who were in the state so early on. Beasley served as a compass for the richness of the African American legacy in California. Through her, I found John Grider, who became the compelling centerpiece of my research, but he was only one part of the larger legacy that Beasley's research helped me to find. She wrote about a number of African Americans central to North Bay history. Many came during the 1850s, while others, including Grider, were here in the 1840s.

I was captivated when I learned that one interview brought Beasley to the North Bay. In the fall of 1914, Beasley "hastened" to Vallejo to interview John Grider after she learned the aging veteran of the Bear Flag Revolt of 1846 was still very much alive. In September of that year, Grider—believed to be the last surviving member of the Bear Flag incident—was honored at a huge Admission Day celebration held in Vallejo. He was eighty-eight years old at the time.

Following the Grider interview, Beasley visited Dr. Platon Vallejo, the son of General Mariano Guadalupe Vallejo, the city's namesake. She was curious to learn what Dr. Vallejo remembered about the June 14, 1846 event, though he had been a child at the time. Although General Vallejo was long gone by the time of this interview, she hoped Dr. Vallejo could give her some insight into what his father thought of the Bear Flag incident, which had ultimately resulted in his arrest.

I believe the interview with Dr. Vallejo gave Beasley a true sense of the kind of leader that his father had been. Dr. Vallejo showed Beasley his father's writings, books, and memorabilia, and Beasley wrote favorably of the Vallejo family. She commended General Vallejo for his positive attitude toward African Americans, stating that "he always voted for the best interest for the Negro while a member of the First California Legislature."

Beasley was the first African American woman to serve as a writer for a general circulation newspaper. Following publication of *The Negro Trail Blazers of California*, Beasley wrote feature stories for *The Oakland Tribune*. These articles focused on black leaders and their contributions and achievements. These feature articles would eventually lead to Beasley's popular column *Activities Among Negroes*, a regular Sunday feature that would last for nearly ten years.

Beasley's columns were often relegated to the back pages of the *Tribune* along with columns on scouting, high school activities, and ads for women's dress patterns. Placement of Beasley's columns did not deter their popularity among Bay Area African Americans.

Logo of Delilah L. Beasley's *Oakland Tribune* column.

Activities Among Negroes was packed with the latest news on black achievements and triumphs. In a period when black men and women were derided or ignored by the larger press, Beasley sought to shine a positive light on their rightful and well earned place in society. Beasley covered people and events in the North Bay. In a December 7, 1930 column she recounted a twenty-fifth anniversary celebration of the California Federation of Colored Women's Clubs held in Oakland.

"Among the out-of-town guests was Mrs. L.J. Williams of Vallejo, who for many years has served as treasurer for the state's organization," Beasley wrote.

In a November 3, 1929 column Beasley wrote of the Vallejo's NAACP triumph in getting a Solano County judge to close down the Vallejo Industrial and Normal School, a school that local black leaders had opposed for years because the school, they argued, represented self-imposed segregation.

Although many authors have quoted Beasley regarding early California history, there has been relatively little written about her personally. However, the late Tarea Hall Pittman, an Oakland civil rights activist, worked with Beasley on various women's club matters. Pittman said Beasley, who never married, was once engaged to Captain Charles Young, the first African American colonel in the U.S. Army and the third to graduate from West Point.[2] One book, *Delilah Leontium Beasley: Oakland's Crusading Journalist,* by Lorraine J. Crouchett, delved into Beasley's activism as a member of numerous organizations, including her work with women's groups that concentrated on the plight of black women.

Beasley died at the Fairmont Hospital in San Leandro, California, on the morning of August 17, 1934. Her funeral was held at St. Francis De Sales Catholic Church in Oakland. At a service the night before her funeral, members of the Delilah L. Beasley Club, a social and civic organization, served as ushers. The author and activist is buried in St. Mary's Cemetery, one of Oakland's oldest cemeteries. Although she was a woman who spent nearly a lifetime with words, her simple, black granite headstone is marked: Beasley, Delilah L. 1871–1934.

---

2 Tarea Hall Pittman, in an interview recorded in the mid-seventies for the Regional Oral History Collection at the University of California at Berkeley.

Delilah L. Beasley is buried in St. Mary's Cemetery
in Oakland. Courtesy Clarence Payne.

John Grider:
A Bear Flag Veteran

On one of my earliest visits to the Vallejo Naval and Historical Museum, Museum Director Jim Kern showed me a photo of the Vallejo Society of California Pioneers. There, in the far left corner of the photo, was the lone African American of the group. "His name is John Grider. Do you know anything about him?" Jim asked. While I had heard of John Grider, until that moment I had never seen his likeness. I caught my breath. Staring out from the faded photo was John Grider, his handsome face reflecting pride.

The Society of Vallejo Pioneers. John Grider is the tiny figure bottom left. Courtesy of the Vallejo Naval and Historical Museum.

THE BEAR FLAG REVOLT OF 1846

More than 160 years before, Grider was one of a group of American settlers who, on the morning of June 14, 1846, took part in an event at Sonoma that launched the struggle for California's statehood. The Bear Flag Revolt, as the events surrounding that date have come to be known, was key to the American takeover of Mexican territory on the Pacific Coast.

On that summer's day, a small, ragtag band of Americans captured the Sonoma County fortress owned by General Mariano Guadalupe Vallejo, who was considered the military power under Mexican rule. The number of Americans who participated is still open to debate. Some historians have estimated the number at thirty-three, while others have said there were only twenty-five.

The group arrested Vallejo, who stayed in jail at Sutter's Fort at Sacramento for more than two months. Shortly after Vallejo's arrest, the Americans lowered the Mexican flag in the Sonoma Plaza and raised the Bear Flag in its place. The party had chosen the Bear Flag because it symbolized the group's fierce determination to rule the western frontier. For twenty-six days—from June 14 through July 9—the Bear Flag Republic was a separate and distinct nation, complete with its own flag and president. On June 17, the fifty-year-old, Massachusetts-born William B. Ide proclaimed the former Mexican province as the California Republic.

Unknown to the Bear Flaggers, the United States government had already declared war on Mexico. John D. Sloat, who was in command of the Pacific fleet, had sailed to California after receiving word that the United States had declared war on the Mexican government. The small band of Bear Flaggers joined forces with the larger, better-equipped Americans. On July 7, Sloat raised the United States flag at Monterey, and the Bear Flag was replaced with the stars and stripes.

Even though short-lived, the Bear Flag Republic paved the way for the United States' struggle to take control of the

Pacific Coast—a move that would eventually lead to California statehood.

This is the original California Bear Flag that was raised on June 14, 1846 at Sonoma. The flag, which was in the possession of the Society of California Pioneers, was destroyed in the Great San Francisco Earthquake and Fire in 1906.

Despite the many published histories of the people and events of the Bear Flag Party extolling the actions of white settlers, scant mention is made of the African American men who were there. Only three of the black men associated with the Bear Flag incident, Jacob Dodson, James Duff, and "Ben," a servant of Lieutenant Archibald Gillespie, received some documentation. It was not until Beasley's 1914 interview with John Grider that the names of other African American men who participated in the incident were mentioned. Grider said there were at least four additional black men — including himself — who were Bear Flag Party members present during the revolt. Those men included Charles G. Gains, Billy Gaston, and Joseph McAfee.[3]

3   Information on the lives of Gains, Gaston, and Lieutenant Gillespie's servant "Ben" is not readily available. Dodson, who was free born, served as a scout for expeditions by U.S. Army Captain John C. Fremont into Western territory in the 1840s. A native of Washington DC, he was about eighteen years old when he accompanied Fremont, known as the "The Pathfinder," on one of several expeditions into the western frontier.

A BEAR FLAG VETERAN'S STORY

John Grider, who came to the North Bay around 1845, was
a veteran of the June 1846 Bear Flag Revolt at Sonoma. He
is the lone African American on Vallejo's Society of Pioneers.
Courtesy of Vallejo Naval and Historical Museum.

Dodson eventually returned east. James Duff, along with McAfee, Dodson, and "Ben," accompanied Fremont on his 1844 expedition. His party traveled up through San Francisco, and by 1846 they were in Sonoma, the site of the impending showdown with the Mexican government. Duff eventually settled in Mariposa County where he lived until he was ninety-three years old. Joseph McAfee, according to the 1860 federal census, settled in Benicia, where he worked as a hotel servant. By 1870, McAfee had moved to Santa Cruz.

Early in my research, I realized Grider had been in Vallejo for a long time—nearly 65 years—and I needed to know more. With Beasley's book in hand, I reread her interview with him. In it, he described his role in the Bear Flag Revolt and how he'd found the paint for the flag, which had been designed by William L. Todd, nephew of Abraham Lincoln's wife, Mary Todd Lincoln. Grider had also served as flag bearer following the incident. However, he told Beasley that the rebellion "didn't amount to much."

I knew I had to find out more about this man who worked in downtown Vallejo—an area I have known all my life. At this stage in my research, I realized there were other African Americans in the North Bay during the nineteenth century. Where would I look? Guy Washington of the National Park Service Network to Freedom project suggested old documents such as census records. Guy, who had reminded me of Grider's connection to Vallejo during a previous conversation, pointed to other vital records, including property deeds and birth, marriage, and death certificates. "Black people purchased property, they married, voted and died ... so there are records somewhere," Guy assured me. I admit I was skeptical of finding information on early African Americans in local records.

GRIDER SETTLES IN

Grider was about twenty years old when he came to California through Mexico in 1845 with his owner, Major George H. Wyatt.[4] Other men in Wyatt's group included Dick Gardner and Major James Burney. Grider and the Wyatt party originally came to California from Silver (probably Sevier) County, Tennessee. Wyatt and party may have accompanied an early exploration party led by U. S. Army Captain John Charles Fremont, a topographer

---

4   Vallejo resident Bill Stevens said in an article in the *Solano Republican* about a week after Grider's death that he had known the Bear Flag veteran for a number of years and had an "accurate account of his (Grider) life's story." Stevens said Grider had once told him he was enslaved to a man named Wyatt and had "crossed the plains to secure his freedom."

assigned to map the Western Territory on behalf of the United States government.

By 1849, the state's gold rush was in full swing, and Wyatt's group, including Grider, headed to Calaveras County in the Sierra foothills. While the lure of gold at Murphy's Diggings would bring the shrewd businessman Wyatt riches, Grider's mind no doubt was set on freedom. Grider was a horse trainer for the Wyatt party, and he worked as a hostler most of his long work life. His skills as an excellent horseman made him invaluable

While in Calaveras County, Wyatt was elected recorder, or alcalde, at Murphy's Camp.[5] As alcalde, Wyatt was the law. By 1850, Murphy's Camp was overcrowded and one of the most successful gold mines. Leonard Withington Noyes, an eastern businessman who made his way west in search of gold in 1849, derisively wrote that Wyatt "had a lot of niggers and southern friends who were of course to be favored" for their choice in gold claims. Noyes also wrote that Wyatt "profited to the extent of two dollars for each claim registered."

Wyatt's time in the mines, due in large part to the labor of Grider and the other African American miners, proved lucrative. Within two years of settling in the area in 1850, Wyatt acquired fifty properties in the newly created town of Vallejo. Grider's work paid for his and his mother's freedom. Beasley wrote how Grider—who was set free in 1850—"paid Major Wyatt $800 to bring his mother (Caroline) to California." Upon his mother's arrival, Grider purchased a home for her in Marysville, where she spent the rest of her life. By the end of that year, Wyatt—who was sometimes called the "first white resident" of Vallejo—had built the Central (or Wyatt's) Hotel. He opened a livery stable with business partner John Brownlie, and Grider would work at the Virginia Street stable for several years.

---

5   From the diary of Leonard Withington Noyes.

GRIDER IN VALLEJO

Grider Jno, hostler George
Higson

Detail from 1869 Vallejo City Directory listing John Grider.
Courtesy the Vallejo Naval and Historical Museum.

By the mid-1850s, Wyatt had sold his share of the livery
stable to John Brownlie and moved to the Central Valley, but
Grider remained in Vallejo. He "bedded" at the Capitol Hotel,
located at the foot of Virginia Street. During the early days of the
city, Grider was a familiar sight as he drove his six-horse wagon
down Georgia Street to the wharves where he helped load wheat
and hay on the schooners docked there. Grider also worked as
a veterinary surgeon, a skill worth its weight in gold in an era
dependent on horses and other animals. F. W. Derrick, one of
the last surviving Pony Express riders when he died in 1938 at
age ninety-six, worked with Grider for ten years at the Brownlie
stable. According to Derrick, there was "no kinder-hearted man or
better man ever than 'Black John' Grider." He added that Grider,
who stood at 5'-9", "was one of the finest roughriders I ever knew."
He said Grider often drove the livery rigs into the bay at the foot
of Capitol Street where he would swim the workhorses to remove
mud from their day's work. Derrick would watch as Grider "drove
a big buckskin horse named Don from John Brownlie's stable into
the bay clear out from the foot of Capitol Street.[6] The horse swam
around Virginia and Georgia streets wharves and came to the foot
of York Street."[7] Grider's horsemanship was also on display when
he and a man named Stewart "would ride wild horses in the lower
block of Georgia Street" during the Fourth of July celebrations.[8]

Throughout his long work life, Grider, who had no known

---

6   See Vallejo map in appendix.
7   F. W. Derrick, from John Grider's December 1924 obituary.
8   Mike Dervin, from John Grider's December 1924 obituary.

family except his mother, worked for various livery stables owned by Henry Connolly and George Higson or as a laborer on area ranches and farms.[9] As a laborer, Grider worked for a farmer named Henry Hannibal, who owned land at the Fleming Ranch, now the Flemingtowne area. Henry Hannibal and his brother, Charles, are listed as mulattoes in the 1860 and 1870 censuses.

From there, Grider went to work punching cattle on a ranch located at White Sulphur Springs Valley, with its towering eucalyptus trees that backed up to craggy hills. Today the area is Blue Rock Springs Park, an area where I picnicked with my family as a child.

In the 1880s, Grider went to work for Vallejo Steam Laundry in Vallejo's downtown. It is believed he ended his work career there, in the late 1890s or early 1900s.

FINDING FREEDOM IN A "FREE STATE"

State of California
Office of the Secretary of State

The undersigned, Secretary of State of the State of California and Keeper of the Archives and Seal thereof, hereby certifies that the foregoing printed law is a true copy of an original Act now on file in this Office entitled "An Act respecting Fugitives from labor and slaves brought into this State prior to her admission into the Union."

Witnesseth my hand and the seal of State impressed on said printed law this twenty-ninth day of January A.D. 1853

Wm. Van Voorhies
Sec. of State

California's Fugitive Slave Act was passed in Vallejo, the state capitol, in 1852. Courtesy of Vallejo Naval and Historical Museum.

---

9   For a time Grider worked at The Point farm, which extended from Glen Cove to South Vallejo.

In January 1852, California Assemblyman Henry A. Crabb introduced the Fugitive Slave Law into the California Assembly, then located at California's third state capital, Vallejo.[10] The law, which mirrored the federal Fugitive Slave Act passed in 1850, made it illegal for slaves to run away from their owners in California. The California legislation became law in April 1852.

One can only imagine what Grider, who was twenty-six at the time, thought as he came into contact with these men who surely left their horses and carriages with him at the Virginia Street livery stable where he worked. Being a black man in such tenuous times and with California's uncertain laws regarding slavery, it's almost certain Grider wanted only to be invisible to some of the legislators, especially those with sympathies toward the south. I'm almost sure he knew these lawmakers were creating laws that touched the lives of so many black people. No doubt Grider knew these men, some pro-slavery, held power over him and the lives of hundreds of African American men, women, and children who now populated California.

While Grider had purchased his freedom in 1850 with money he earned in the mines of Calaveras County, his status as a free man was not clear. California was a contradiction. It had been declared a free state, yet there were scores of enslaved black men, women, and children in the North Bay in the 1840s, 1850s, and 1860s. In September 1855, a Missouri-born slave, Adam Willis, was set free in a Benicia courtroom, but Missouri-born Nancy Geary was brought to Solano County in bondage in the 1860s.

To many slave owners and bondsmen, a free state was no more than words on paper. Large numbers of southerners had come to the new state with their property in tow—cattle, furniture, and slaves. Some of these white southerners grabbed for power as soon as they settled in California and were elected to local, regional, and statewide offices. Many early white settlers needed slaves to work the gold fields and clear newly acquired land, and no

---

10   Vallejo served as the California state capitol from 1851 through 1853.

amount of weak legislation banning slavery in the Golden State was going to get in their way.

Early settlers, who knew slavery was big business in the south, wanted to capitalize on the "peculiar institution" in California. Take, for example, the January 15, 1846 deed that details the sale of at least 35 men, women, and children in St. Helena—with a profit of more than $9,500. In 1850, of the twenty-one African Americans listed in the Solano County census, fourteen "were slaves [from] Missouri and have contracted to work in the state and then be set free after two years."[11] Although the men were under "contract," legal agreements between whites and blacks during the 1850s weren't worth the paper they were written on. Black people had no legal standing in California courts. Slave owners could and did renege on contracts or promises made with blacks because state laws banned African American testimony in legal matters. What happened to those fourteen African American men who were enslaved in Solano and who were promised freedom in two years is unknown.

In 1851, two white southerners eyed the Napa Valley and the Feather River as possible locations for a slave colony. The intent of the colony was to supply labor to the gold fields. The inhabitants of the colony would work the land and mine the gold fields under the direction of "educated and intelligent masters." On December 7, 1851, James Gadsen, a native of Charleston, South Carolina who had once served under Andrew Jackson in the war against the Seminoles, wrote a letter to General Thomas Jefferson Green exploring the possibilities for this North Bay slave colony. Green, a native North Carolinian, had come to California in 1849, bringing a number of slaves with him. Gadsen, in his letter, explained that the Feather River area was a good choice and that Napa Valley "may be more desirable, but it is occupied ... held high and too far I fear from the gold region."[12] Other

---

11   Solono County 1850 census index.
12   James Gadsen in a letter to Gen. Thomas Jefferson Green, December 7, 1851.

areas considered for colonization were San Diego and Monterey. However, the plan never materialized.

Many African Americans fled California around 1858, choosing to go to British Columbia rather than risk being enslaved. The exodus had been prompted by a series of events that occurred leading up to that year. The state's black population had been anxiously watching a number of events with trepidation. A major case occurred in January 1858 when eighteen-year-old Archy Lee, a slave, appeared before Judge Robert Robinson in Sacramento after he was arrested for escaping from his owner, Charles Stovall. Young Lee, in the company of his owner Stovall, came to California in 1857. Stovall, after an unsuccessful stay in California, decided to return to his home state of Mississippi, taking Lee with him. Lee, however, had other plans. He ran away. Stovall later found Lee and had him arrested. On January 26, Judge Robinson decided in Lee's favor and set him free. Lee was immediately rearrested on a warrant issued by state Supreme Court justice David Terry, who subsequently found in Stovall's favor.

In February of 1858, just as Stovall and Lee were preparing to return south by ship, Lee was arrested once again, only this time it was by his supporters. His case was brought to district court in San Francisco, where the previous court ruling was overturned and Lee was set free once again. Before Lee could leave the courtroom, he was arrested by a federal marshal. This time the Lee case was brought before the United States Commissioner William Penn Johnson, who ruled that Lee did not cross state lines to seek freedom and, therefore, the 1850 Fugitive Slave Act did not apply. Lee was at last free.

The state's black population, however, could not relax. Within weeks of the Lee case, new state laws were being introduced to ban blacks and Asians from the state. White men were increasingly angered by competition from African Americans and Asians, who, they believed, were undermining their ability to make money in the Sierra placer mines. In March of 1858, a state law was introduced banning black people from the state. The proposed legislation would require those blacks who were here to register with the government and carry registration papers at all times. While the proposed bill passed the assembly handily, it was defeated in the senate by parliamentary maneuvering.

While the anti-immigration law was defeated in 1858, the state's black community believed that it might come up again in the next session. Hundreds of blacks, fearing the possibility of enslavement, prepared to leave the state. Word was out that gold had been struck in the Fraser River area of British Columbia. Black people set their sights on Canada and headed north. [13]

Grider, like so many others, chose to remain in the North Bay. Many of the blacks who stayed were ever vigilant in watching for signs of slavery in the region. In one instance, Beasley notes that Grider encountered black men who were enslaved on a Napa ranch. Beasley offers no details of how it was done but explained that Grider's discovery was brought to the attention of the Rev. Thomas Starr King, a well-known San Francisco minister and abolitionist, who helped to secure the freedom of these men. Starr King came to San Francisco in 1860 and died there on March 4, 1864.

THE BEAR FLAG VETERAN FINALLY RECOGNIZED

At the dawn of a new century, Grider, whose life had depended on horses, was now aging. The first automobiles were starting to appear on the streets of Vallejo. Perhaps it was a fitting turn of events for Grider, whose long life had been touched by so many major events.

---

13 Myrtle Holloman in a *Modesto Bee* article in 1974 said her great grandfather, Howard Estes, was part of a party of 600 men, women, and children from Northern California, Oregon, and Washington who chose to relocate to Canada in 1858. Holloman said black families sold their farms, cattle, and other possessions before making the journey north. Most of the women and children in the party traveled on board the steamer ship *Brother Jonathan* out of San Francisco. The men traveled by horseback and wagon train, many driving their remaining cattle to their new home.

On September 9, 1914, during a huge Admission Day celebration held in Vallejo, Grider's contribution to the state was recognized.[14] Even though a Vallejo newspaper writer misspelled Grider's name—calling him John Cryder— the article noted that the Bear Flag veteran, riding in a special automobile, was among those "cheered all along the route."[15] Grider "was treated royally and accorded every honor pertaining to the hospitality of the city."[16] The tribute by more than forty thousand people who had converged on Vallejo that day was not lost on African Americans throughout the Bay Area.

The *Western Outlook*, an African American newspaper based in San Francisco, also made note of this event.[17] It stated that "the only survivor of the Bear Flag Party rode in solitary state in an automobile, a vehicle his wildest imagination never pictured in the strenuous days of California's fight for membership into the Union." To know that Grider—who had mostly only known horses and wagons and who no doubt lived a very simple existence—was being hailed by the city as one of the last remaining Bear Flag veterans was a bittersweet recognition. In 1916, an ailing Grider moved into the Fairfield County Hospital. Back then, the county hospital was considered a combination hospital and "poorhouse" for indigent and sickly county residents.

John Grider died just three days before Christmas of 1924. The acknowledgement in the local newspaper was impressive—a long, front-page article, "Interesting Sketch of a Negro Pioneer," was heartfelt and informative. It was in Grider's death that many Vallejoans first learned of this former slave's contributions and connection to both the state and city. Although Grider had been

---

14 The Admission Day celebration was hosted by the Vallejo Parlor No. 71, Native Sons and Daughters of the Golden West.

15 From the September 11, 1914, *Vallejo Times Herald*.

16 George Van Blake, another early African American resident of Vallejo, in a letter to Beasley, following the parade.

17 While the October 7, 1914 edition of *The Western Outlook* in which the article appeared is no longer available, Beasley quoted the article in her book.

recognized as a Vallejo pioneer (a rare recognition of an African American) and was feted during the 1914 Admissions Day Parade in Vallejo, it is doubtful that many people in Vallejo knew the extent of Grider's importance.

Grider, whose death certificate said he died of "arteria sclerosis," was buried on December 23, 1924, the day after his death. He is buried in a common grave in the Suisun Fairfield Cemetery in Fairfield. His final resting place is the rear of the cemetery—what was at one time the pauper's grave area.

New Beginnings

EDUCATION: ANOTHER DREAM REALIZED

This circa 1885 photo detail shows an unknown African American student at a Vallejo grade school. Courtesy Vallejo Naval and Historical Museum.

On a crisp fall day in the late 1850s, Nancy, James, and George Holman rushed to a waterfront hotel in downtown Vallejo where they attended class.[18] Freedom, education, and the right to vote were the holy trinity for African Americans during that period. The Holman children were among several black children who attended the one-room school for colored children. George and Isabel Holman, who were no doubt born into slavery in their native Missouri, were determined to see their children educated.

---

18 The Vallejo school for black children was housed in one room of the United States Hotel at 21–22 Maine Street.

Grider, who lived and worked only a short distance from Vallejo's colored school, probably watched the Holmans and other black children as they made their way to class. Unable to read or write, Grider no doubt placed his hopes and dreams in this new generation.

Like most African American schools of that period, Vallejo's earliest "colored school" was most likely established and funded by black parents. A number of African Americans were trained by and had attended schools in northeastern cities. The most educated person in the community was most likely encouraged to teach the students. Such was the case for other North Bay black schools in Napa, Petaluma, and Santa Rosa. Members of the black community in Napa placed an advertisement seeking "a colored teacher [male or female] to take charge of a school in Napa city with a good recommendation. Apply to J. S. Hatton, Main Street, Napa City." [19]

The issue of how school districts would deal with local black children was ongoing. In 1871, a Fairfield assistant teacher with the consent of the school board taught six black children only after the dismissal of her "regular" pupils. This practice was also done in Santa Rosa. "We only have one colored scholar and he is taught by one of the public school teachers at odd hours."[20] The teacher was paid an additional fifteen dollars a month for his services.

Many early black schools had close ties with churches in the area; Napa's African American school was probably connected to the African Methodist Episcopal church, which had a Sabbath school.[21] Petaluma's African American school, located at Fifth Street, south of D Street, was started in early 1864 and was one of a few publicly funded colored schools in the state. Rev.

---

19 From the August 13, 1869, edition of *The Elevator*.
20 From an April 5, 1877 article in the *Santa Rosa Times*.
21 The Napa African Methodist Episcopal church was located on Washington Street. An 1875 article in a Napa newspaper reported that Fannie Hackett was the teacher.

Peter Killingsworth and George W. Miller founded this school. Newspapers such as the *Petaluma Argus* railed against the publicly funded Petaluma black school and urged school trustees to abolish the school. In one article, the *Argus* claimed that Petaluma was the "only school district west of the Rocky Mountains that maintained a colored school for less than ten pupils" and said Petaluma was the "laughingstock of the whole country." The other publicly funded schools were in San Francisco, Sacramento, Marysville, San Jose, and Stockton.[22]

Black families who didn't reside in the towns and cities where there were black schools had only a few choices when it came to education. Those options were limited to starting their own private schools, sending their children to board with family and friends in areas where there were state-funded schools, or doing without an education. The third option was out of the question. The parents, many of whom were former slaves who'd been denied an education, were determined to provide their children with this opportunity. The fight was a protracted one, but North Bay African Americans from Santa Rosa, Vallejo, Napa, and Petaluma played important roles in the battle.

In 1865, on a warm summer day, John Richards and other prominent North Bay African Americans beamed as students in Santa Rosa's black school showed off their grammar school skills to an audience gathered for a semi-annual examination. The students were tested in diction, reading, grammar, geography, arithmetic, and penmanship. That happy day was an attempt to show the white visitors that Santa Rosa's black children were both intelligent and worthy of education.[23] In the audience for this big day was the Rev. Peter Killingsworth, minister of Petaluma's African Methodist Episcopal church, as well as two prominent white members of the community: Santa Rosa's superintendent

---

22 In 1864, John Swett, the state superintendent of public schools said California had 831 black school-age children.

23 As described by teacher Amos Johnson in a July 3, 1865 letter to *The Elevator* newspaper.

of schools, Charles G. Ames, and William Churchman, a county judge.

Up until that point, Santa Rosa's school board had refused to fund the district's black school. State law, which denied black children access to white schools, allowed a school district to set up separate educational facilities for black children if the district had ten or more African American school-age children. In 1865, Santa Rosa had eight black school age children, two short of the required number.

In a follow-up letter addressed to "The friends of education in California" a few days after the examination exercises at the black school, County Judge Churchman wrote that the exhibition proved that Santa Rosa's black population was determined "to improve their minds and prepare their children for the responsible positions portended by passing events." He acknowledged he had visited "few primary schools among our own color [white] where the same proficiency and progress during the short interval, was manifested." Churchman went on to add that the skills of both the children and teacher showed "remarkable aptness." However, he avoided any mention of funding or assistance for the black students or school.[24]

So as he had in years before, John Richards, a well-to-do barber, paid thirty dollars a month to hire a teacher for the town's black children, including his own two, Ella and Frank. The true injustice of the board's refusal to fund a black school was that Richards—who owned a number of properties in Santa Rosa—paid seventy dollars in taxes that year to the county. In essence, he and other blacks who owned property financed the education of white children while their own were expected to do without.

Well into the 1870s, similar stories were being played out in counties throughout California. It was more than apparent that many whites were determined to block attempts to publicly fund education for black children. Their determination, however, was

24   Churchman's letter, dated July 3, 1865, and printed in *The Elevator* along with Amos Johnson's letter.

matched by African Americans parents who were determined to see their children educated.

What can only be described as an early attempt at school integration took place in Napa in March 1871. Several unnamed African American girls walked into a Saturday afternoon writing class where they attempted to enroll. "They seated themselves among the white trash," one article noted. The teacher, in an effort to prevent white students from leaving, reluctantly asked the black girls to leave. "They consented and equanimity was restored" the article explained. Making the black girls leave was troubling to the teacher, whose name was listed only as Hoffman. He said he was not accustomed to teaching separate classes for whites and blacks.

But the article made it clear there would be no mixing of the races at the writing school. "We don't consider it any credit to himself [Hoffman] … if he taught in communities where the social equality of the races was established; nor do we consider it any credit to the colored people of any section to insist upon associating themselves with whites." The writer went on to say that he hoped "our colored people will find pleasure and profit enough in the society of their kind and in the schools and churches kept up for their benefit."

An editorial in *The Pacific Appeal*, a San Francisco-based newspaper aimed at the African American community, blasted California's segregated school system and implored African Americans to take legal action against school districts and if necessary to take their cases to the state and nation's highest courts. To have children "driven from the free schools in each county for which they are taxed in common with other citizens is becoming unbearable," the editorial explained.

In 1872, a statewide educational committee of California's top African American leaders issued a call for black people to push for educational rights. "The time has now arrived when we should vigorously press our claims for the educational facilities for our children whom the laws grant us, and for which the state makes manifest provisions," noted the educational committee's report.

North Bay African Americans J. Looney, John R. Landeway, Charles Gibson, John Richards, and William Veasey helped raise funds to mount an uphill legal fight against California's restrictive and racist education laws. Santa Rosa still had not enrolled black children into its school system by 1876.[25] By the end of the 1860s and early 1870s, Vallejo's school board was offering financial assistance to its separate African American school. However, even when districts provided financial assistance to black schools, the conditions were less than ideal.

Obviously incensed that Petaluma continued to educate black children, one writer challenged school districts in Santa Rosa and Healdsburg: "Petaluma is not the only place in Sonoma County in which there are colored children. Will our contemporaries in Santa Rosa and Healdsburg please inform the public what course is pursued in regards to the education of the colored youngsters who form part of their respective communities?" On July 3, 1874, Vallejo's school board voted to abolish its black school, thus "allowing" African American students to enroll in the general public school. However, this desegregation was more about money than justice—by eliminating the teacher's salary and the "heavy rents" paid for the separate facility, the cash-strapped district was able to save on costs. This was not true integration.

Just days after the Vallejo school district voted to abolish the black school, the *Vallejo Evening Chronicle* took special pains to soothe white parents' fears. "Now if the colored children are put in the white school, they are, we have been assured by the Secretary of the Board of Education, to be seated in one part of each room by themselves."

The fight for the educational rights of African American children was far from over—the children were enrolled in elementary school, but higher learning remained inaccessible. In 1877, Henry Jones attempted to enroll his son in a Petaluma

25 From the November 24, 1876 edition of the *Argus*.

high school. The principal told Jones, "No colored child should be admitted as long as I am principal of the school."

It would be thirty-two years after Jones attempted to enroll his son in high school before the first known African American students in the North Bay Area would graduate from high school. Vallejo's Ellsworth Courtney completed Vallejo High School in 1909, while Mazie Strickland graduated from a Napa grammar school around the same time.

Ellsworth Courtney, top row center, is pictured in this 1905 Vallejo middle school photograph. Young Courtney was one of the first known African American students to graduate from Vallejo High School in 1909. Courtesy Vallejo Naval and Historical Museum.

Mazie Strickland, second row, far right, graduated from a Napa high school around 1911. Courtesy of the late Madeline Ontis.

EARLY ENTREPRENEURS: NORTH BAY
BLACKS ESTABLISH LOCAL ROOTS

As the smell of freshly roasted coffee and smoked bacon beckoned waiting customers, Thomas Moore Grove finished last-minute preparations before opening his Georgia Street restaurant on an early winter morning in 1867. For nearly a year, the Jamaican-born Grove, a friend of John Grider, had operated his popular restaurant at 66 Georgia Street in Vallejo. The restaurant, just steps from the town's bustling waterfront, served a ravenous clientele of mariners, teamsters, and other workers who helped make up the local early workforce.

Grove operated his restaurant well into the 1880s.[26] He was part of the North Bay's small but important cadre of African Americans who owned businesses from the 1860s through 1900s.

---

26 According to the Vallejo City Directory.

From the late 1860s through the 1870s, downtown Vallejo had at least six black-owned businesses in a three-block radius.

As early as the 1860s, Bay Area newspapers were touting Vallejo as an excellent locale for African Americans to start businesses and purchase property. "This is a flourishing little city, its harbor second to none on the coast. It promises in many ways to vie with San Francisco. I would advise our friends who are desirous of accumulating wealth to visit this place and secure property or go in business and grow with the city, as it is bound to thrive."[27]

These early business pioneers were the exceptions in the nineteenth century labor force. In post-Emancipation America, most black men and women were relegated to low skilled and poorly paid jobs. Still, black men and women established barbershops, bathhouses, hotels, restaurants, and blacksmith businesses. Black women also worked for themselves, establishing dressmaking businesses, hair salons, and restaurants; many hired out their services as nursemaids and midwives.

From the 1860s on, blacks in Vallejo, Benicia, Fairfield, Suisun, Napa, Santa Rosa, and Petaluma found their business niche. In the mid-to-late-1800s, black men formed a near monopoly in the barber business. Many took full advantage of the opportunity, which afforded them economic independence and social status within the black community.

27　From *The Elevator*, the San Francisco–based weekly that served the African American community.

Barbershop Owners

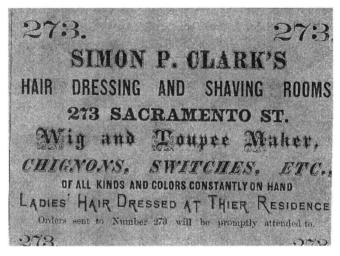

This ad for a barbershop owned by Simon P. Clarke
(whose name was misspelled in the ad) appeared
in an 1870 Vallejo City Directory.

Simon P. Clarke was one of several Vallejo barbershop owners; his hairdressing business was at 273 Sacramento Street. In the 1870 Vallejo directory, Clarke took out a handsome, half-page advertisement. Clarke's services catered to men and women, including hairdressing, shaving, and wig and toupee making. Women could choose from "chignons and switches ... of all kinds and colors" that were always on hand. Elsewhere in downtown Vallejo, John R. Landeway, Wilson Dixon, Harry Williams, and G.W. Hawkins owned and operated barbershops.[28]

In Benicia, George Williams owned a barbershop on First Street, between D and E streets. Joseph H. Cason also owned a Benicia barbershop. In Napa, Joseph S. Hatton and his father Edward

---

28 John R. Landeway's shop was at 170 ½ Georgia Street. Dixon operated a shop on Santa Clara Street between Georgia and Virginia streets. Harry Williams kept his shop at 136 Georgia Street. At one point, George W. Hawkins owned a shop on Georgia Street and later moved his business to the Carquinez Hotel in South Vallejo. All are listed in the 1870 Vallejo City Directory.

ran barbershops on Main Street. The Hattons were prominent in African American leadership circles both in the North Bay and statewide. William Christopher also owned a barbershop on Napa's Main Street. Frederick Sparrow was yet another Napa barber who operated his own shop on Main Street. From 1860 through the early 1870s, George W. Miller owned a barbershop in Petaluma. In Suisun, Margaret Smith advertised her skills in creating "ladies' curls and braids in a superior manner" at her shop.

Edward Hutton, of Silveyville (later renamed Dixon) owned the only barbershop in town. The shop was located in the center of town, opposite Silvey's Hotel, the town's principal hotel. Hutton's shop was within "rods of the express and post offices." He advertised in several editions of *The Elevator* in 1868, seeking to sell the barbershop and its "good will," along with all of its "necessary appliances for conducting the business." "The shop is doing a business of nearly Three Thousand Dollars a year and the running expenses are very light." Along with the barbershop, Hutton, a native of Washington DC, also offered for sale a separate cottage (suitable for a family and measuring 18 by 24 feet), barn, stable house, and horses for a total of $1,100. As part of the sale, Hutton offered two bay horses "suitable for carriages . . . or family uses, a mare and two colts, one sired by Dashaway that promises to be speedy." Hutton was "compelled to sell" because he planned to leave the country.

Restaurant Owners

Nancy Geary lived in Dixon for more than 40 years. She came to Dixon, then known as Silveyville, in the 1860s. Courtesy Dixon Public Library.

In the late 1800s, Dixon's Nancy Geary, dubbed the "Ice Cream Lady" by local townspeople, operated an ice cream parlor at the Mayes Building. Geary was born in Missouri and came to California in the 1860s and was well known in the Dixon area because of her business. The popular shop eventually turned into a restaurant. A September 2, 1898 Dixon newspaper noted, "Mrs. Nancy Geary is prepared to furnish a wholesome meal at the corner of First Street and will treat her patrons well."[29]

In Vacaville, Will Stepp owned and operated the Starr Restaurant.

Other Successful Entrepreneurs

In the 1860s and 1870s, Clayton Jones ran a wheelwright shop in Suisun and built horse carriages and wagons and repaired wagon wheels for area residents. William H. Stewart, another Suisun entrepreneur, ran a restaurant, lodging house, barbershop, and bathing salon on Main Street a short distance away from Margaret Smith's hair dressing shop for women. In the 1860s and 1870s, Napa's William Bailey earned a living as a blacksmith, while Charles Stewart owned a "dancing house" and later a hotel.

29 Geary had two children, Jefferson and Frank. Her son Jefferson died early. By 1900, Frank worked at Mare Island where he was one of the first electricians at the navy yard. Nancy Geary is listed in the 1870, 1880, 1900, and 1910 censuses.

> ### STEWART'S
> ## Restaurant & Lodging House
> #### Adjoining the Roberts House, Suisun City,
> #### Entrance at the Barber Shop.
>
> ---
>
> ### STEWART'S
> ## Barber Shop & Bathing Saloon
> #### Connected with the Restaurant.
>
> WHERE none but the best are employed.—
> Give him a call. Prices moderate, and
> satisfaction guaranteed.
> ap24 :   WM. H. STEWART.

This advertisement in *The Elevator* in the late
1860s features a Suisun business.

Sonoma County was the home of John Richards, one of
the North Bay's most prominent and wealthy business owners.
Richards owned businesses in Santa Rosa, Ukiah, and Lakeport.
In 1867, he was appointed vice president of the Phoenixonian
Institute, a San Jose-based organization that was at the forefront
of the fight for equal educational rights for blacks. The institute,
organized in 1863, grew out of African American efforts to
establish a private high school for black children. The 1870 census
said Richards worth was more than $10,000, an amazing amount
for anyone, regardless of race.

In the late 1800s and early 1900s, Vallejo could boast an
African American chiropodist (foot doctor) who served the larger
community. Dr. Rodgers (his first name is unknown) came to
California in 1863 from the West Indies after being "connected
with the Navy" and had learned his profession at his home in the
West Indies.[30]

While Napa and Sonoma counties would see a sharp decline
in their black communities and black business ownerships
during the late 1800s, African American entrepreneurs in Vallejo
remained. As the black population in Vallejo grew, lured by jobs
at Mare Island during the pre- and post-WWI years, black men

---

30   According to Delilah L. Beasley's *The Negro Trail Blazers of California*

and women expanded their business opportunities. In the early 1900s, C.C. Courtney and his two sons, Charles and Ellsworth, owned taxi services in downtown Vallejo. D.G. Corbin, a well-to-do businessman and the first president of the Vallejo NAACP, owned numerous properties throughout the city that he rented out. Nightclubs, boarding houses, and restaurants, including a lunch counter operated by the Second Baptist Church at Capitol and Branciforte streets, were open for business

CIVIL WAR AND EMANCIPATION: "WE ARE PERMITTED TO BEHOLD THE DAWN"

Just two years after the Civil War broke out thousands of miles away, forty-nine year old Catherine Jackson was purchasing a home in Benicia. But what had to be on Jackson's mind was the war that raged in the south she once called home. After all, Jackson, who was a slave when she came to California in the 1850, had left five children behind in Missouri. Their welfare had to weigh heavily on her heart and mind. Jackson's story was not unlike many blacks who had come to Californian in the 1840s and 1850s. As slaves, they had no choice but to come to California and leave their loved ones.

By 1863, when Jackson purchased her Benicia home from J. P. Van Hagan, she was free. The purchase of her home was no doubt in preparation for the day when her children—whom she'd last seen in her native Missouri—would reunite as a family. Some years later, her daughter Mary Ann Lane and a son would join her; however, it is not known if her other children ever reunited with her.

The outcome of the War Between the States was as important to North Bay African Americans as it was to any slave in the south. They eagerly sought news of battles on southern soil and the progress being made by Union soldiers. The news of the Civil War was dispensed in a number of ways in the Bay Area. Daily and weekly newspapers, both white and black, brought news from the battlefront. Letters from relatives back home told

California African Americans how they were faring. Those men and women who couldn't read listened to preachers, barbers, businessmen, and friends, who would pass on whatever they had heard. Church pastors passed on news from their pulpits, and stewards aboard Bay Area steamer ships that plied local waterways passed on information they received from passengers and other ship personnel.

The Pacific Appeal, the black weekly, brought news of colored troops and their efforts during the war. In an 1862 news story in the *Pacific Appeal,* the issue of arming African American troops to serve in the Union was raised. Local African Americans like John Grider signed up for the Union Draft in August 1863. Although thirty-seven at the time, Grider's age is listed as twenty-eight. Grider was not drafted. Henry Holmes, who would eventually move to Petaluma in the early 1870s, saw battle in the Civil War, serving in the 13th Regiment Colored Troops Heavy Artillery.

Other articles, such as one in the summer of 1862, brought news of former Vallejo resident and first commander of Mare Island, Commodore David Farragut who "confiscated ... three thousand slaves employed on the Vicksburg (Mississippi) canal."

Hundreds of people from throughout Northern California attended the joyous Emancipation Jubilee celebrating the freeing of millions of black men, women, and children. The event, held at Platts Hall in San Francisco was no doubt the most important day of so many lives. North Bay men who helped to plan the Grand Jubilee celebration included Erastus Briscoe (Suisun), S. P. Clanton (Benicia), and Edward Hatton (Napa).

"This is a day of thanksgiving and rejoicing to us," said J. B. Sanderson, the well-known educator who gave the keynote address for the jubilee that day. Speaking on behalf of the five thousand black people who now called California home, Sanderson said the day President Lincoln signed the Emancipation Proclamation (January 1, 1863) was a day "our father desired to see, and for which we have prayed. They died without the sight—we are permitted to behold the dawn—ordering the light of the advancing day of freedom to our race."

Well into the twentieth century, Emancipation Day celebrations—always held on the first day of the year—continued to be one of the most important days within the black community. Huge celebrations were held in cities and towns large and small. Area residents would help plan these celebrations.

Leading the Way

NORTH BAY AFRICAN AMERICANS PLAY KEY ROLES AT COLORED CONVENTIONS

When forty-nine prominent African American men gathered in the St. Andrews AME Church in Sacramento in November of 1855, they helped launch the state's first civil rights movement. This first California Colored Convention was one of four such meetings that would be held over the next ten years in 1856, 1857, and 1865.

These gatherings, which included delegates from Solano, Napa, and Sonoma counties, focused on the political and economic plight of the state's African American population, which had grown steadily following the gold rush. In these conventions, delegates hammered out strategies to fight laws that denied African Americans education, the right to testify against whites, and the right to purchase property.

The 1855 meeting in Sacramento helped not only to assess the broad talents of those gathered but also served as a forum to address the mistreatment and second-class status that blacks experienced statewide. North Bay residents who attended the

37

conventions were Edward Hatton, H. Pennington, Elisha Banks, and Isaac Johnson who represented the North Bay counties. The 1856 convention, which also was held in Sacramento, and the 1857 gathering, which was held in San Francisco, continued to address many of the same issues raised at the first gathering. North Bay black leaders, such as George W. Miller of Petaluma and C. H. Gibson of Napa, played key roles in the 1865 convention and served on various committees.

On August 14, 1865, black residents of Solano County gathered in Benicia to elect a delegate to the October convention. S. P. Clanton presided over the August meeting, while W. H. Miller served as secretary. The electing committee declared they wanted "to send a man whom we feel confident will lend himself to no 'clique' ... but heartily exert for all measures ... to the good of our whole people in the commonwealth." The group elected N. E. Speights (F.G. Barbadoes served as his proxy). Miller, also a delegate to the 1865 convention, played a key role at that gathering, as did William H. Christopher, who represented Napa and served as the convention's assistant secretary.

At the October gathering, the Committee on Statistical Information presented surveys of black communities throughout California, including the North Bay. These surveys helped measure black progress both economically and socially. Napa's survey showed that black people owned $51,000 in real estate and other property. Sonoma reported that African Americans in the county owned $25,000 in property. Sonoma County's survey listed 55 adults and 20 children. There were 10 black farmers, 2 carpenters, 2 blacksmiths, 7 barbers, and 12 general laborers. The survey reported one church and one schoolhouse. Solano County did not present a report.

The 1865 convention, held a few months after the end of the Civil War, was heavy with meaning for many of the delegates. Shortly after 10 AM on October 28, the Reverend Peter Killingsworth, a delegate from Petaluma and pastor of the Union AME Church there, stood and with great emotion addressed those gathered in the church sanctuary. As the audience listened with rapt attention, the man serving as chaplain of the convention shared his poignant story of being enslaved for sixty-two of his seventy years. Eight years earlier, Killingsworth explained, he had purchased his and his wife's freedom while living in Atlanta, Georgia. He'd paid $3,000. He and his wife then migrated to California, where she died upon arrival. Killingsworth said that he took solace in the knowledge that while his wife was no longer alive, "her bones lie in the free soil of El Dorado."

BLACK MEN GET THE VOTE: "WE HAVE SOMETHING TO LIVE FOR"

Frederick Sparrow of Napa was one of the first African Americans in the North Bay to register to vote in 1870. Photo courtesy of the Civil Rights Movement Veterans.

In April 1870, Frederick A. Sparrow strode the short distance from his home to the Napa County Courthouse where he registered to vote for the first time. Days before, the Fifteenth Amendment, which granted African American men the right to vote, had been passed. Sparrow, who had long waited for this day, was ready. What a momentous day this had to be for twenty-seven-year-old Sparrow, who became one of the first black men in the North Bay to register to vote.[31] Sparrow bore the hopes of so many African Americans who had long dreamed of this day.

In early 1870, *The Elevator* requested and received from agents and readers throughout California lists of African American men who, with the passage of the Fifteenth Amendment, would be eligible to vote. In Napa, Sparrow was selected to symbolically represent the township's black community. Sparrow was educated, having been a student in one of the first schools for black children established in the 1850s. He owned a barbershop at 52 Main Street, and he and his twenty-two-year-old wife, Alice, were the parents of three children. There could be no better representative of the black community to test this uncharted territory.

After registering to vote on April 8, 1870, Bear Flag Veteran Joseph McAfee summed up what black men across the nation were no doubt feeling: "We have got something to live for, and we feel good; we are men now, and will act like men; Uncle Sam will find us good citizens all the time."

Except for the day blacks got word they were free, the right to vote was the most important day of their lives. Freedom and the right to vote gave blacks greater choices, or at least they hoped so. Despite the injustices and cruelty many African Americans faced during this harsh time, these early pioneers had an abiding faith in the system and themselves. They believed if they would do the right thing—vote and become educated—then their efforts would be rewarded and full citizenship would be theirs.

Hundreds of Napa residents, black and white, gathered at Napa Hall on April 11, 1870 to mark the ratification of the Fifteenth Amendment. Napa's celebration was one of several held throughout Northern California. North Bay black people hosted events in Napa

---

31   *The Elevator* reported that in addition to Sparrow, Wm. H. Lee of Stockton also registered to vote.

and Santa Rosa, complete with speakers, dinner, music, and dancing. While many blacks in Vallejo attended the Napa ceremony, a large contingent boarded a steamer ship to attend a huge celebration in San Francisco. One paper noted "quite a number of 'fifteenth amendments' [colored people] visited San Francisco from Vallejo to take part in yesterday's celebration."[32] The article went on to say the procession numbered about fifteen hundred persons.

"The exercises were impressive and interesting; one hundred guns were fired from Russian Hill and orations were made by the Rev. Messrs Hillary, Morgan, and Anderson. In the evening, balls and parties were given, which fittingly closed the colored men's festivities in celebration of the ratification of the Fifteenth Amendment."

In the North Bay, a local newspaper announced "the colored citizens of Napa will jubilee on Monday next. They intend to fire 100 guns ... and have some interesting exercises."[33] And jubilee they did. On the day of the celebration, Napa's black residents gathered for a full day of activities, including a speech given by the Rev. William R. Hillary, one of the state's most important black leaders:

Our colored citizens celebrated the ratification of the Fifteenth Amendment to the Constitution of the United States in this town on Tuesday last in a highly creditable ... and orderly manner. The program consisted of the firing of 100 guns at 11 a.m. at Napa Hall and a social re-union at Quinlan and Williams' Hall in the evening.

The orator of the day, Rev. William R. Hillary, a full-blooded citizen of African descent and of South Carolina nativity, is a natural orator of fine personal appearance and of liberal education. His delivery is easy, his language good and his style florid, yet not devoid of true eloquence.

His oration was a grand literary success and one which is

32 *The Vallejo Evening Chronicle*, April 6, 1870.
33 *Vallejo Evening Chronicle*, April 11, 1870.

*seldom equaled by of greater pretensions and of whiter skins.
The hall was crowded with ladies and gentlemen of all parties
and the orator was frequently applauded by his people. The
hall was elegantly festooned with flags and everything passed
decently and in order.*

The Solano County Great Register listed a number of black
men who registered to vote in the 1870s through the 1890s. These
were: John Grider, George Van Blake, and his son William, John
Henry Maddox, Pink Brown, John Balfour Clark, John William
Stanton, Henry Edward Mussenden, Benjamin Fann, Adam Willis,
Squire Baker, George Washington Hall, Thomas Moore Grove, and
Edward Curtee.

LEADERSHIP IN PRINCE HALL MASONS
AND OTHER FRATERNAL ORDERS

Equally vital to the development of the early California African
American community was the fraternal orders established shortly
after statehood. Early North Bay African Americans played key
roles in these fraternal and benevolent societies that proliferated
throughout Northern California from the 1850s on.

Records show that North Bay black residents were leaders
in the state's earliest fraternal orders, whose membership rolls
read like a who's who of nineteenth century California African
American leadership.

According to an account from a June 26, 1865 *Elevator*
newspaper article, Masons from the Bay Area converged on
Benicia to celebrate St. John's Day, a Masonic holiday. Members
of Olive Branch No. 4, and Werthington Lodge No. 7, who
came from throughout the Bay Area, chartered "the large and
commodious" *San Antonio* steamer for an excursion to Benicia.
The celebrants were addressed by William H. Yates and William
H. Hall, "the silver tongued orator of California."

On their return from Benicia, the excursion party passed
Mare Island, where a French freighter laying over at the Navy

Yard for repairs honored them. The freighter "gracefully lowered and raised their flags three times, with our flags answering ... our bands playing patriotic airs and all hands cheering lustily." It was a powerful moment; even if their fellow Americans ignored them, at least another country—as represented by the crew aboard this French ship—honored their existence.

Many of the North Bay Area's prominent African Americans were associated with the lodges. Napa's Edward and Joseph Hatton were founding members of Laurel Lodge No. 6 in Marysville and were active at the highest levels in the fraternal order's statewide governing body. Simon P. Clarke, a Vallejo businessman who owned a Sacramento Street barbershop in the 1870s and 1880s, was an active member of Victoria Lodge No 3. He served as Grand Secretary of Prince Hall Grand Lodge and was a Royal Arch Mason. In 1923, L. J. William of Vallejo was selected grand lecturer of the state's Grand Lodge.

Thomas Moore Grove, a longtime Vallejo resident and businessman who owned one of Vallejo's earliest restaurants in the 1860s, served as deputy grand master of the state grand lodge in 1883 and 1884. John R. Landeway, another Vallejo resident and businessman served as worshipful master of Victoria Lodge No. 3 in 1887 and 1888.

Charles H. Tinsley of Vallejo served as grand master of Hannibal Lodge No. 1, San Francisco. Hannibal Lodge, established June 12, 1852, is the oldest lodge in the California Prince Hall Masonic Order and still exists. Tinsley served as most worshipful grand master of the state's grand lodge in 1907–09.

By the early 1900s, Vallejo's expanding black community started to address the need for organizations such as fraternal orders and benevolent societies. These groups were the backbone of African American communities throughout the United States. By 1915, the Grand United Order of Odd Fellows and the Knights of Pythias were organized.

Black Spanish-American War veterans who helped organize the fraternal orders had been active for years and by 1916–17 had built a two-story hall at 1209 Georgia Street. This hall, which still exists today, would become the center of Vallejo's black community for decades to come.

Strict racial and social mores of the day separated blacks and whites. Such separation was the norm, so white Spanish-American War veterans in Vallejo met on Georgia Street in the city's downtown, while black veterans met in their hall in what was then outside the city's limit on Georgia Street.

Built during the height of the First World War in the classical revival style then popular, the lodge building was impressive when first erected. The streets surrounding the structure were unpaved. Local residents who attended social gatherings at the hall either walked or rode horse and carriage to the building. The two-story structure served as a community center for Vallejo's growing black community and was used for meetings, dances, and dinners. The hall, with its honey-colored wood floor and its period wainscoting, brought pride to African Americans during those years marked by war and racial conflicts.

In many ways, 1209 Georgia Street stood as a testament to the war veterans—mostly Buffalo Soldiers, who had come to Vallejo more than a decade before and formed the backbone of Vallejo's twentieth century black community. They helped not only to build the Georgia Street hall but also established churches, fraternal orders, benevolent societies, civil rights organizations, and businesses that made an indelible mark on Vallejo.

The original deed on the building (there have only been two) revealed Vallejo's connection with national military history. Named as trustees on the July 28, 1916 document are William Fryson, Brooks Johnston, John L. Malone, E. U. Moore, Alexander Morrow, George W. Posey, and W.C. Wyne.

Prince Hall Masons Firma Lodge No. 27, Vallejo was originally built around 1915 or 1916 for African American veterans of the Spanish-American War. Courtesy Prince Hall F&AM Firma Lodge No. 27, Vallejo.

The men, the deed indicated, were members of the Captain Charles Young Camp 6, Department of the Columbia, United Spanish War Veterans. In 1884, Charles Young became the third African American to graduate from West Point and was commissioned as one of a few African American military officers. He served in the segregated army of the late nineteenth and early twentieth centuries. Young's assignments included the Philippines, Haiti, Liberia, Mexico, and the United States.

J. L. Malone, like these unidentified Buffalo Soldiers, served
at Yosemite and Sequoia National Parks at the turn of the
twentieth century. Malone was one of the founders of Vallejo's
Second Baptist Church. Courtesy National Park Service.

Young, who hailed from Springfield, Ohio (as did Delilah
L. Beasley), was stationed at the San Francisco Presidio where he
was in charge of black troops known as Buffalo Soldiers. In 1903,
Young led an escort of troops for President Theodore Roosevelt.
Six days later, Young led a contingent of Buffalo Soldiers on a 323-
mile trek by horseback from the Presidio to Sequoia National Park,
where Young had been assigned to serve as acting superintendent
of the national park. [34]

John L. Malone, whose name is also on the Firma Lodge
deed, served directly under Young at Sequoia National Park.
Malone and his wife, Sophia, helped found Vallejo's Second
Baptist Church in 1907. The church's first organizational meeting
was held in the Malone's home on Carolina Street.

---

34 As noted earlier, Young reportedly was engaged to Delilah Beasley, though
    he eventually married another woman in the early 1900s. It is interesting
    to note, however, that Young was stationed at Presidio and the Sequoia
    National Park just a few years before Beasley relocated to California.

L. J. Williams, a founding member of Firma Lodge No. 27, Vallejo.
Courtesy, Prince Hall F&AM, Firma Lodge No. 27, Vallejo.

Within two years of its construction, the Georgia Street building became the meeting spot for newly created fraternal order of the Prince Hall Masons Free and Accepted Masons, Firma Lodge 27.

On June 5, 1918, L J. Williams, Alex Taylor, and J. E. Berry met in the Spanish-American War Veteran's Hall on Georgia Street and helped organize Firma Lodge No. 27. The local fraternal order's name, Firma Lodge, was more than appropriate the members believed. This new lodge with its determined leadership was established on a "firm foundation."

Though the building has changed hands only once in its ninety-three years, many groups have found a place within it. In 1942, the building was leased to the United Service Organization, or the USO, for the use and entertainment of black servicemen, servicewomen, and the community. In the late 1940s, Friendship Baptist Church met in the building and the Omega Boys Club held some of their early meeting in the lodge. During the early 1950s, a credit union established by the Prince Hall Masons had an office there. A few years later, Golden State Mutual Insurance opened its first Vallejo office in the building. Other fraternal orders and their female auxiliaries also met at the lodge, including the Order of the Eastern Star, the Heroines of Jericho, and the Grand United Order of the Odd Fellows, The Household of Ruth, and the Knights of Pythias.

On June 6, 1946, Firma Lodge purchased the building from the Veterans and Auxiliary Hall Association, headed by President James M. Owens and Financial Secretary E. U. Moore.

On June 9, 1956, Firma Lodge No. 27 reached a major milestone and held its official mortgage burning ceremony just ten years following the official purchase of the building.

With few changes, the building still stands. Its original features, like its well-worn wooden floors, steep wooden stairs, and large meeting room, would still be familiar to those early members who first met in the building in 1916.

Firma Lodge No. 27 served as the pioneer organization of the Masonic family in Vallejo. Out of Firma Lodge other lodges and chapters formed, including Fidelus Chapter, Order of Eastern Star, in 1923; Amicus Lodge No. 48 and Harmony Court, both organized in 1944; in 1953, both George W. Posey Lodge No. 77, and Oriental Chapter were organized.

While some of the fraternal orders are no longer in existence, Firma Lodge No. 27 still meets at 1209 Georgia Street and keeps alive a legacy established nearly a century ago.

We Were Here: Profiles of North Bay African Americans

Black people first came to western America in the 1500s, traveling with Spanish explorers who were determined to build a new empire for their country. These men and women of African descent traveled with explorers like Sir Francis Drake, who came to San Francisco Bay in 1579. Twenty-six of the first forty-six settlers of Los Angeles were black or mulatto. Residents of African descent made up more than 19.3 percent of Santa Barbara in 1785 and by 1790 were 15 percent of San Francisco's population.

Black people who came to the North Bay in the 1840s and 1850s were largely natives of slave-holding states, such as Missouri, Kentucky, Tennessee, and Virginia. But there were also large numbers who hailed from Pennsylvania, Massachusetts, New Jersey, and New York. Most of these early settlers were freeborn. But there were men and women who came to the North Bay from throughout the African Diaspora—including the West Indies, the United Kingdom, and Africa; forging new lives in a new land was their commonality.

ADAM WILLIS

Although California was admitted into the Union as a free state in 1850, for many early African Americans living in the state, "free" was just another word. Adam Willis, who was about 23 when he arrived in the Mexican territory that would become the state of California, is a perfect example.

Born a slave in Missouri, Willis came west with his owner, Major Singleton Vaughn, in 1846. Leaving his family behind in Missouri, Vaughn accompanied by Willis made their way west, settling first in what would later become the town of Woodland. A short time later Vaughn and Willis moved to Benicia, Solano County's first town.

By the early 1850s, a now established Vaughn was Solano's second county tax assessor. It was time, Vaughn decided, to bring his family west. That task was put in the hands of Willis, by now in his late twenties. In the early 1850s, Willis returned to Missouri to fetch the Vaughn family, perhaps with assurances that he would be set free upon his return. Willis was set free on September 27, 1855 in a Benicia courtroom. Willis was thirty-one years old.

The emancipation document, written in the elegant script of the period, records that Willis paid $1 for his freedom. Because African Americans were considered property, the transaction was finalized by a deed. The 151-year-old document is believed to be the first of its kind to be found in Solano County.[35] In part, the document reads that Singleton Vaughn "released from slavery, liberated, manumitted and set free ... his Negro man named Adam."

Following his emancipation, Willis moved to the Suisun-Fairfield area where he forged a new life for himself. For several years, Willis served as a cook for Captain Josiah Wing, the founder of Suisun City. Willis also worked as a cook for a variety of other area families as well as for the Solano County Hospital.

---

35 The deed (book H. page 520) is part of the permanent records housed in the Solano County Archives in Fairfield.

52

To all whom it may concern
Be it Known that I Singleton Vaughn
of the county of Solano in the State
of California for divers good causes
and considerations me thereunto moving as also in further consideration of
the sum of One Dollar current and
lawful money of the United States
of America to me in hand paid have
released from Slavary liberated manumitted and set free and by these pres
ent do hereby release from Slavary liberate
manumit and set free my negro man
named Adam being of the age of
twenty six years and able to work and
gain a sufficient livelihood and
maintenance and him the said
Adam I do declare to be henceforth
free manumitted and discharged
from all manner of Servitude or Service to me my heirs Executors or ad-
ministrators forever
        In Witness Whereof I have
hereunto set my hand and seal
this 25th day of September A.D 1855

                Singleton Vaughn

State of California
County of Solano ⟩ss On this twenty
seventh day of September A.D 1855
personally appeared before me Joseph
P Vaughn County Clerk and Ex Officio
Clerk of the County Court in and for
Solano County in said State Singleton
Vaughn personally known to me to be
the Individual described in and who
executed the foregoing instrument of
writing and acknowledged that he
executed the same freely and volun-
tarily for the uses and purposes
therein mentioned

This manumission paper set Benicia resident Adam Willis free on
September 27, 1855. Courtesy of the Solano County Archives.

51

Information Wanted ad placed by Adam Willis. *The Elevator.*

Twelve years after being set free, Willis placed an ad in *The Elevator.* The ad, in the October 11, 1867 edition read:

Information Wanted

Marian Willis, who when last heard from, was in Ray County, Missouri. Any information of her whereabouts will be thankfully received by her brother, Adam Willis at Suisun City, California.

Springfield Republican and Zion Standard of New York, please copy one month and send bill to The Elevator.

By 1880, the Solano County census listed Mary A. (no doubt Marian) Fann as living in Suisun with her brother, Adam Willis. Also living in the household were Willis' adult nephews, nieces, and grandnephews. By 1900, the family would grow even larger with the addition of two grandnieces.

The advertisement that reunited Willis and his sister Mary Ann was not unusual following the end of slavery. Long after emancipation, African American newspapers throughout the nation printed notices of family members seeking information of spouses, parents, children, and siblings who had left the south with their white owners; many newspapers continued to publish such notices well into the 1900s. Many African American families, torn apart by the horrors of slavery, were never reunited.

THE LANDEWAY FAMILY

Early records and a poignant two-page letter written nearly eighty years ago provide a clear picture of how one African American family arrived in Vallejo in the mid-1800s. In a September 1930 letter to the San Francisco-based Standard Oil Company, seventy-four-year-old Elizabeth Landeway Venable requested a 49er pioneer certificate. It is not clear why Venable wrote Standard Oil Company regarding the pioneer certificate, although it may have been part of a promotional campaign that was sponsored by the company. Venable wrote that she could prove her family's state residency back to 1852 and wanted the certificate to pass on to her grandson, Albert Kingsbury, who was going to be two years old in November 1930. In addition to Venable's letter, city directories, newspaper articles, census, and Masonic records provide additional details about the Landeway family.

Venable's mother, Anne Fuller Landeway, first arrived in California in 1852 as a stewardess aboard an eastern ship that came by way of Cape Horn to San Francisco. While in San Francisco, Anne Fuller met John R. (J. R.) Landeway, who also worked as a steward. In September 1855, the couple wed. Within the next year, the Landeways returned east to Jersey City, New Jersey, where Elizabeth was born on June 12, 1856.

In their return east, Venable said her parents chose not to travel by way of Cape Horn. Instead, "they traveled cross the Isthmus of Panama by way of burros." The 1860 census lists the Landeways as living in Jersey City, New Jersey.

The family returned to California in 1863, choosing again to sail around Cape Horn. They settled in Oroville, where Elizabeth's brother William was born. While it is not clear what year the family moved to the North Bay, by 1870 the census lists the Landeways as living in Vallejo. That year's census listed Elizabeth, fourteen, and brother William, ten, "in school."

While the early part of J. R. Landeway's life was devoted to the sea (the 1860 census lists Laneway as a seaman), he worked as a barber in Vallejo for many years. His barbershop was located in the 100 block of Georgia Street during the 1870s. The Landeways lived above the barbershop for many years, but by the 1880s the family lived in the 800 block of Marin Street.

J. R. Landeway was actively involved in issues and events impacting the state's African American community. By the 1860s, Landeway was a member of a statewide education committee that agitated for educational opportunities for African American children. He and fellow Vallejo barber Wilson Dixon represented Solano County.

Landeway was an active Republican and in October 1872, he hosted a Bay Area delegation of the Grant Invincibles. The group came to Vallejo via steamer ship to participate in a torchlight procession and rally for the re-election of President Ulysses S. Grant. The gathering included speech making at Eureka Hall, fireworks, and a parade.

Elizabeth, who was married twice, first wed in Vallejo in the centennial year of 1876 to George Taylor, a native of the West Indies. The 1880 census lists them as living in Vallejo with their four-year-old daughter, Mary.

GEORGE AND ELIZABETH VAN BLAKE

By the early 1870s, perhaps encouraged by their relatives, John and Anne Landeway, George and Elizabeth "Deborah" Van Blake moved to the West Coast. The Van Blakes were early members of Vallejo's African American community, coming to the North Bay from Pittsfield, Massachusetts, in the early 1870s.

The 1870 census lists Van Blake, thirty-one, as living in Pittsfield with wife, Elizabeth, twenty-nine, and son William, ten. In Pittsfield, Van Blake worked as a coachman. Young William, who was born in New Jersey, is listed as "in school."

Not long after his arrival, Van Blake took a janitor's position with the Vallejo Savings and Commercial Bank located at the northwest corner of Georgia and Sacramento streets. The Van Blakes owned a home at 208 Pennsylvania Street. Tragically, their son William died of unknown causes at age twenty-nine in October 1892.

While there is little written about George Van Blake, brief glimpses into his life reveals a man of great pride. In 1895, he joined the newly created Afro American League and represented Vallejo as a delegate to their San Francisco convention.

In a 1914 letter to the *Western Outlook,* a black San Francisco newspaper, Van Blake paid tribute to his longtime friend John Grider, the Bear Flag veteran, noting that Grider had been honored during a huge Admission Day parade held that year in Vallejo. The 1876 Great Register shows Van Blake and Grider registering at the same time. Van Blake was literate, while Grider could neither read nor write. Van Blake no doubt helped Grider decipher the registration form and any other items that needed to be signed.

George Van Blake died of heart problems on March 10, 1917, seven years before Grider. The Van Blakes were highly thought of in early Vallejo. This was evident in an obituary that appeared on the front page of *The Vallejo Evening Chronicle* marking Elizabeth Van Blake's death on July 23, 1918:

Mrs. Geo. Van Blake, colored, widow of the late George Van Blake, for many years janitor of the Vallejo Commercial Bank, and a resident of the city for over half a century, passed away at her home this afternoon. So far as is known she had no immediate relatives but many friends will mourn her passing."

Elizabeth Caviel, wife of A.B. Caviel, cared for Mrs. Van Blake during the last days of her life.[36] Mrs. Van Blake left more than $1,200 in her estate, which a Solano County court judge awarded to her cousin Elizabeth Landeway Venable of Oakland on March 25, 1920.

---

36 The Caviels had two daughters, Ethel and Julia. They lived at 112 Pennsylvania Street, a block away from the Van Blakes.

GRAFTON T. BROWN

Grafton T. Brown. Courtesy of the California Historical Society.

While it is not clear whether lithographer and artist Grafton T. Brown lived in the North Bay area, evidence of his presence in Sonoma County is documented in his sketches of area buildings and landscapes. Those sketches by the talented and prolific Brown included a rendering of the Santa Rosa Academy, a view of Santa Rosa, and the Santa Rosa House. These, as well as other works by Brown, who was born of free parentage in Pennsylvania in 1841, are part of the Robert B. Honeyman Collection of Early California and Western American Pictorial Material in the Bancroft Library at UC Berkeley.

Brown came to Northern California in the late 1850s. The 1860 census lists the nineteen-year-old Brown as a resident of Sacramento. Brown's talent caught the eye of printmakers who relied on artists to execute drawings that documented the settlements, gold rush towns, and ranches that were spreading throughout the region.

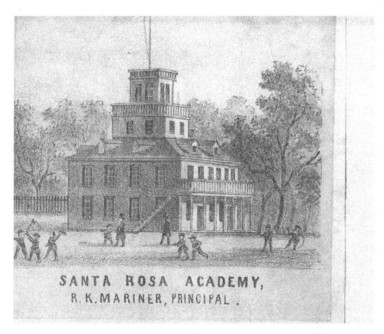

SANTA ROSA ACADEMY,
R. K. MARINER, PRINCIPAL.

Grafton T. Brown drew this sketch of the Santa Rosa Academy
in the 1860s. Courtesy the Bancroft Library, U.C. Berkeley.

Brown's work also served to document and chronicle buildings, land, and people in a manner that was nearly photograph perfect. Kuchel & Dresel, Brown's employer, put the view of Santa Rosa drawn by Brown on stone. Britton & Co. printed the sketch, possibly in 1859. Charles C. Kuchel died in 1865, and by 1867 Brown had taken over the company, which was at 543 Clay Street in San Francisco. Brown's San Francisco business flourished until 1879 when he sold the business.

Few men, black or white, earned a living off their artistic skills. That Brown, an African American in the nineteenth century, could do it for nearly his entire life was impressive. By 1882, Brown left the Bay Area for Vancouver, British Columbia where it's believed he was a member of a geological survey party. Brown later moved to Portland, Oregon, where he began to focus on paintings. By the end of 1892, Brown lived in St. Paul, Minnesota, where he worked as a draftsman. He died in 1918.

The New Century Brings New Hopes and New Concerns for North Bay Black Residents

As Solano County pioneers John Grider, Adam Willis, and Nancy Geary marked their seventy-plus years of life, a new millennium was dawning. In 1900, Grider was 74 years old and was believed to be working at the Vallejo Steam Laundry on Pennsylvania Street. The lone African American listed among the Vallejo Society of California Pioneers—a distinction given to men who came to the state before 1849—Grider lived in near obscurity during his seventy years in Vallejo. Willis, who was about seventy-six, was still employed and working as a cook for the Fairfield County Hospital. Nancy Geary still made her home in Dixon. By 1900, Joseph S. Hatton and the Hatton clan had left Napa and relocated to Marysville where Hatton would remain until his death in 1918.

POPULATION SHIFTS

During that same period, African American men, many veterans of the Spanish-American War, converged on Vallejo and brought with them leadership skills that would become the foundation of Vallejo's black community. Increasing numbers of blacks had moved to Vallejo seeking work at the Mare Island Navy Yard (later renamed the Mare Island Naval Shipyard). There were numerous work opportunities at the navy yard as a result of the 1898 Spanish-American War. *The Vallejo Evening Chronicle* reported in its April 8, 1920 edition that Vallejo's population had gone from 11,340 people to 16,853, a 48 percent jump overall and a 50 percent increase in the town's black population. These migration patterns of African Americans between the Spanish-American War and World War I were proof that Vallejo, with its military base that promised work, was viewed as a viable locale for black folks.

A large number of African American men, many former Army veterans or Buffalo Soldiers, flocked to Vallejo. James Williams, a lifelong Vallejo resident, grew up hearing the stories of the black Army veterans who came to Vallejo in the early 1900s. Williams, who still lives in Vallejo, knew many of these veterans. Williams' father, Peter, worked at Mare Island in the 1920 and told a story of how many Buffalo Soldiers came to Vallejo. According to the elder Williams, an Army official who commanded the black soldiers was concerned about their treatment following the Spanish-American war. Many of these men were raised in the South and did not want to return to their home states.

The Army officer reasoned that these men, who were stationed at the Presidio in San Francisco, would need work and a place to settle. The Army officer, according to Williams, contacted cities throughout California seeking a new home for his men. Vallejo, with its navy yard, was contacted. The Army officer never received a reply, which he took as a positive sign. He sent his former charges to Vallejo.

These Army veterans had served in the 9th and 10th Cavalry and the 24th and 25th Infantry and many had seen war in the Philippines and Cuba. Those veterans included: W. C. Wyne, William Fryson, Brooks Johnston, John L. Malone, E.U. Moore, Alexander Morrow, George W. Posey, James Owens, J.C. Turner, J. R. "Jock" Taylor, Alex Taylor, Charles Courtney, William Wiggins, and James Jeter. Sylvester Spriggs and Marion Hill served in the navy during the Spanish-American War.

James Owens, a Buffalo Soldier in the 9th Cavalry, served in the Spanish American War. He was a founding member of the Vallejo branch of the NAACP, Firma Lodge (Masons) and was Vallejo's first known black building contractors. Courtesy Dolores Owens Cofer.

George W. Posey, center, a former Buffalo Soldier, pictured with his wife and an unknown friend, was a prominent member of Vallejo's early twentieth century African American community. They are standing in front of the Posey's Illinois Street home. Courtesy Catherine Fulcher.

By 1900, the black population had declined substantially in most North Bay towns and cities. But Vallejo was undergoing a sharp increase in the numbers of African Americans moving in. According to the Federal Census of 1900, the black population in Solano County saw the biggest upsurge between 1900 and 1910, when the numbers of blacks and mulattos went from 54 to 210 people.[37] The population increases created strains on a city that had long outgrown its housing supply. While there was no designated area where African Americans were forced to live in the early twentieth century, Vallejo's black population largely lived in boarding houses that lined Capitol and Branciforte streets. In the second decade of the twentieth century, black families bought property and built houses in other areas of Vallejo, including Illinois Street, Denio, Sacramento, and Carolina streets.

Sonoma County posted a slight increase in black people from 1900, when the census recorded 23 people of African American descent, 28 in 1910, and 44 in 1920. By the early 1900s, job opportunities were moving to the more populated cities like Vallejo.

VALLEJO'S NEW MIDDLE CLASS

The horse and buggy era was slowly coming to an end and a new breed of young African Americans—many the offspring of former slaves—were moving to the North Bay Area and mostly to Vallejo where there was work and a growing community of African Americas. Shifting job patterns that favored industrialized rather than an agrarian economy was largely the reason for the black population increase in places like Vallejo.

Despite a larger job market, black people struggled to make a living in Vallejo during the early twentieth century; most held low-skilled, low-paying positions and were crowded into the boarding houses that were plentiful on Capitol and Branciforte streets. But there was an emerging, albeit small, black middle class in Vallejo

---

37 Note: The census numbers are not entirely accurate, as they tend to only count heads of household and not children.

that included former teachers from the south whose skills would land them plum positions at Mare Island.

During the first decade of the twentieth century, at least eight African American men served as clerks at Mare Island. That eight African Americans held such positions before 1910 was remarkable. A government clerk's position was coveted by any race during that period. Most government clerk jobs required education; reading and writing skills were essential. A. B. Caviel, Henry S. Amerson, and Charles Toney were schoolteachers in Texas before they moved west and were hired on as clerks at Mare Island. Other black clerks were: H. S. Anderson, E. U. Moore, Eugene C. Berry, William Wiggins, and L. J. Williams. Williams was also the first African American bookkeeper to be hired at Mare Island, around 1905. Frank Geary, the son of Dixon's Nancy Geary, was one of Mare Island's first electricians. The 1900 census lists Geary as an "electro lineman." Marion Hill, a Navy veteran, was a fireman on Mare Island.

These early blacks started to build homes on York, Illinois, Louisiana, Sacramento, and Denio streets at the turn of the twentieth century. James Owens, one of the first black building contractors in Vallejo, built his own home on Denio Street around 1918 and likely helped build numerous other homes in the city. Many other African American-built homes, including several surrounding the Kyles Temple site at Illinois Street at Sonoma Boulevard, still stand. These classic bungalows in the early 1900s, while modest by today's standards, no doubt reflected the lifestyle of a comfortable black middle class whose jobs afforded home ownership and stability. Vallejo could boast enclaves such as neighborhoods on Illinois Street and Louisiana Street off of Broadway Street.

Within months of their arrival this new breed of African Americans, many the children and grandchildren of former slaves, started to build on the foundation of Vallejo's black community that had come before them. Within the first two decades of the twentieth century, Vallejo's black community saw the formation of two churches, fraternal orders, including Prince Hall Masons, and the National Association for the Advancement of Colored People (NAACP). Families were formed, increased numbers of black children were enrolled in local schools, homes were built, and the formation of a strong and viable black community was underway in Vallejo.

THE SO-CALLED FIGHT OF THE CENTURY

The Vallejo African American community celebrated Jack Johnson's (right) victory over Jim Jeffries during the 1910 so-called Fight of the Century.

The famous fight between Jack Johnson and Jim Jeffries, held on July 4, 1910 in Reno, was billed as the "Fight of the Century." Jeffries came out of retirement to prove that a white man was "better than a Negro" by fighting Johnson, the first black world heavyweight champion. Vallejo boxing fans, black and white, gathered in saloons and other meeting spots on Georgia Street for a blow-by-blow description of the fight. "The thrilling story of the great battle will be sent into the *Chronicle* just as fast as the United Press can handle the stuff," reported the July 2, 1910 *Evening Chronicle*.

The powerful Johnson pummeled Jeffries, who had been touted as "The Great White Hope." In the eleventh round, Johnson knocked Jeffries down twice. Before Johnson could knock Jeffries down for a third time, officials stepped in and declared Johnson the victor, fearing possible riots by angry whites. The following article appeared in the *Vallejo Evening Chronicle:*

Victory of Johnson over Jeffries causes great satisfaction to local colored people

The colored people of Vallejo certainly enjoyed Johnson's victory over Jeffries yesterday. Wherever the residents of the local colored colony gathered they were bubbling over with happiness of the pleased expressions on the faces of men and women alike showed that they were grateful over the result. Last evening a party of eight colored sports engaged an automobile and went out for a joy ride, painting the town red during their travels.

It must be said to the credit of the local colored population that there was nothing offensive in their conduct such as the carrying on of colored people in other sections of the country.[38]

Black people could boast of few public victories over whites during the early 1900s. But with the much-awaited contest between Johnson and Jeffries, black people could take vicarious pleasure with each punishing blow from Johnson's fists.

RACIAL TENSIONS INCREASE

Against the backdrop of race riots and racial tensions, Ku Klux Klan chapters sprang up throughout California, including Vallejo, Napa, and other nearby towns. The Klan openly advertised meetings in newspapers like *The Oakland Tribune.* In Napa County, the number of African Americans had dwindled to fifteen according to the 1900 census. The drop in Napa's black population had been noted as early as the 1890s. Bishop J. W. Hood, an African Methodist Episcopal minister, wrote in an 1895 publication marking the one-hundredth year of the AME church that blacks had abandoned Napa some years before.

While the number of blacks there rose slightly to thirty-six in 1910, Napa would never see the thriving African American

---

38   Hundreds of African Americans lost their lives in the wake of Johnson-Jeffries fight.

community it had during the 1880s. By 1920, the number of blacks had dropped to thirty-one.

Personal safety and lack of job opportunities were two of the reasons for the decline. Newspapers were filled with articles about lynchings, beatings, and the rise of racist organizations like the Ku Klux Klan. As the twentieth century dawned, African Americans in ever-increasing numbers turned their sights to cities such as Vallejo, the home of Mare Island Navy Yard. As early as 1902 there was talk of establishing a colony for blacks in Vallejo. A March 22, 1902 article in *The San Francisco Call* noted the "Rev. G. H. Smith, minister of the African Methodist Church, is organizing a colored congregation in this city, and has completed preliminary arrangements for the erection of the church. He stated that all negotiations have been concluded for the establishment of a Negro colony in Vallejo. The colony is coming from North Carolina." African Americans who moved to Vallejo just before and shortly after 1900 were not to be deterred. Many of the newcomers to this area had come from the Deep South and were determined to make the North Bay their new home.

As Vallejo's black population grew so did their demand for social, civic, and religious organizations. One of Vallejo's first formally organized black churches was Second Baptist Church. Prior to the organization of Second Baptist in 1907, black people held church services in private homes or halls. But both the increasing black population, along with an insult, would lead to the founding of Vallejo's first organized black congregation.

Second Baptist Church was formed shortly after blacks attending Cornell Baptist Church (now First Baptist Church) around 1905 were rebuffed from the podium by the white minister. In no uncertain terms the minister said to the congregation that he would be glad when "the colored people" in attendance formed their own church. Even before the insult, a group of African Americans had started the conversation around establishing their own churches. By 1907, the Second Baptist Church was launched and the Rev. J. A. Dennis was elected the church's first minister. Church meetings were initially held in an old building on Sacramento Street. A few years later, the church purchased a building at Branciforte and Capitol where the church remained until 1964.

By 1910, Kyles Temple African Methodist Episcopal Zion Church had formed. The church congregation first met at the Old Labor Temple on Virginia Street. In 1916, the congregation moved into the newly completed Spanish-American War Veterans Hall at 1209 Georgia Street. By 1919, Kyles Temple members had purchased land at the corner of Illinois and Sonoma streets (now Sonoma Boulevard) where they planned to erect their church. The white Methodists planned to build a new church to replace their old sanctuary that had been built in the 1860s. They sold the old wooden structure to the black congregation for about nine hundred dollars. Later that year, the Kyles Temple church was burned to the ground by an arsonist, heightening the racial tensions in the area.

The Vallejo NAACP in the 1900s

FORMATION OF THE VALLEJO NAACP

On a Sunday afternoon in the early spring of 1918, an enthusiastic throng of mostly Vallejo residents joined to form the local branch of the National Association for the Advancement of Colored People. Vallejo's NAACP, with its seventy-one charter members, was among the earliest branches in California and, over the next ninety years, helped shape the political, economic and social future of the county's black community. Mary White Ovington, Archibald Grimke, and Oswald Garrison Villard, national officers of the NAACP and three of the best known names in the early twentieth century civil rights movement, signed Vallejo's endorsement as a branch.[39] Among those who corresponded with the Vallejo branch were civil rights heavyweights of the period, including NAACP National Secretary James Weldon Johnson and Walter White, assistant secretary.

---

39   Archibald Grimke was the nephew of Sarah and Angelina Grimke. Commonly known as the Grimke Sisters, they were staunch abolitionists. Oswald Garrison Villard was the grandson of abolitionist William Lloyd Garrison.

Months before the New York headquarters chartered the Vallejo branch in June 1918, it was evident the Vallejo branch was busy at work. In a March 25, 1918 letter to the NAACP New York headquarters, newly elected branch president D.G. Corbin, a successful Vallejo businessman, wrote that the local branch was not only enthusiastic, they also had "money in the bank."

From its inception, the Vallejo branch launched head on into some of the most important issues facing African Americans during that turbulent period following World War I. Blatant discrimination in housing and employment for the city's approximately two thousand black residents was ongoing. Nationwide, lynchings of African Americans were at an all-time high and bloody race riots swept the nation.

In one of its first actions, the Vallejo branch raised money for Dr. LeRoy Bundy, an aid to Marcus Garvey, the leader of the Universal Negro Improvement Association. In a May 27, 1918 letter from Vallejo branch secretary F. D. Clopton, local members sent word to the national headquarters saying local members were prepared to donate money to the defense fund set up for Bundy, an East St. Louis, Illinois dentist charged with conspiracy stemming from bloody race riots that swept East St. Louis in 1917. In a period of some of the bloodiest race riots of the time, the East St. Louis riot was considered one of the worst.

Bundy had been charged in the deaths of two white police officers killed during the riot. By the end of the day on July 2, 1917, rampaging whites murdered more than one hundred African Americans. Hundreds more were left homeless. But only blacks were arrested and charged with crimes relating to the riot.

Bundy's arrest, subsequent trial, and conviction—he was sentenced to life in prison—earned him celebrity status among African Americans across the nation. While Bundy's conviction was overturned two years after his conviction, the incident mobilized African American fighting blatant racism locally and nationally.

Local issues in a World War I-era Vallejo were the major

focus of the newly formed civil rights group. An overcrowded Vallejo with little housing to spare, increased job competition, and racial tension made for an uneasy co-existence between the races. Evidence of that tension came in the summer of 1919 when the Vallejo NAACP sent a letter to Mare Island Commandant E.L. Beach asking that he reprimand four white sailors who had insulted African American women as they left Sunday church services (no doubt Second Baptist Church) in downtown Vallejo. Specifically, the NAACP asked Beach to protect Vallejo's "colored people from further insult ... especially when the vessels of the new Pacific fleet arrived at the navy yard."

Beach responded by sending a letter to the NAACP, the *Vallejo Evening Chronicle,* and *the Oakland Tribune.* In the *Chronicle* article, Beach said the NAACP asked for his cooperation with the black community in preventing the spread of race riots such as those sweeping the nation that year. Just three days before Beach's response to the Vallejo NAACP, a major riot swept through Chicago, Illinois. That same year other major cities, including Washington DC, Omaha, Nebraska, Charleston, South Carolina, Longview, Texas, Knoxville, Tennessee, and Elaine, Arkansas, saw bloody rioting between whites and blacks, resulting in thousands of lives lost and millions of dollars in property damage.

Rather than respond to the NAACP's assertion regarding the sailors' behavior, Beach chastised the organization for bringing up the issue of possible riots. The commandant advised the NAACP "against any concerted actions in this regard as the one certain way to create discontent was to hold meetings where possibilities and rumors were discussed to the extent that people themselves finally believed them."

Beach, in a condescending tone, assured the NAACP that "the white people of Vallejo are your good friends" and that he did not expect any racial problems in the town because of "the friendly relations" between the two races.

Beach's failure to address the NAACP's claims was an insult to the Vallejo black community, especially in light of similar incidents that involved white sailors and white women. In one Vallejo newspaper account around that same time, Vallejo police arrested two white Mare Island sailors for "annoying a woman and her child and making insulting proposals." Both men were ordered back to their barracks at the navy yard and were given 30-day suspended sentences.

Vallejo's NAACP Addresses the Kyles Temple Burning

Within two years of its formation, Vallejo's NAACP would be called upon to address the torching of the historic Methodist Church that that had been purchased by members of Kyles Temple AME Zion Church. The November 1919 inferno was the culmination of what *The Vallejo Evening Chronicle* called "a spirit of resentment" by white residents of the Sonoma and Illinois street neighborhood. Rumors spread, including one that the historic church would never be placed on its permanent foundation. Even before the historic church was moved to its location, violent attacks against a temporary building erected by the black church members were frequent.

On Sunday mornings, as black church members worshipped, vandals threw rocks at the church and broke windows. In September 1919, vandals made an attempt to burn down the temporary sanctuary but the blaze was extinguished. On one occasion tar was smeared on a church sign, and doors and windows were nailed shut. Frustrated by the attacks and the lack of a police investigation, the NAACP pleaded with Vallejo city officials to assist them in stopping the attacks. In a letter to the national NAACP office, Vallejo branch president D.G. Corbin wrote "the annoyances became so intense it was necessary to appeal to the city officials for protection on numerous occasions." Vallejo city officials ignored the pleas. On November 28, 1919, alarm bells pierced the quiet of a Vallejo morning and alerted local firefighters to a blaze at the corner of Illinois and Sonoma streets. On arrival the firemen found the historic wooden church once owned by the white Methodist Episcopal congregation ablaze.

Both black and white Vallejo residents were outraged by the November arson. Following the destructive fire, Vallejo Mayor James Roney and the Methodist Episcopal pastor Rev. A. B. Gilbert denounced the church burning. "It is a blot on the name of Vallejo for conditions to exist wherein people, whatever their creed or color, are prevented from worshiping God," Roney noted. Two days later, the local newspaper announced that the First Methodist Church had passed a "resolution of regret over the church burning." "The burning is regarded as inconsiderate and heartless." Following the incident, African American men decided it was time to protect their families and property, and some decided to purchase arms.

The Vallejo branch offered the district attorney assistance to help in any way they could. For months, the Solano County District Attorney's Office ignored the NAACP. "The sense of the majority of the Negro people think ... he is uninterested and not friendly ... towards Negroes."

The city council and the two churches raised a reward of more than five hundred dollars for the arrest and conviction of those responsible. After several months of investigation, Vallejo bank official Henry W. Opperman was arrested on second-degree arson charge. A warrant signed by Rev. S.E. Edwards, Kyles Temple pastor, was issued for Opperman, who was indicted by the Solano County Grand Jury.

Even with the arrest of Opperman, a director of the Central National Bank, the Solano County District Attorney was indifferent to the case. Opperman owned a number of properties "in the vicinity" of Kyles Temple. During the trial he was lauded by a number of character witnesses who "testified to the good nature of the defendant." Among those testifying on Opperman's behalf was J. J. Madigan, former Vallejo mayor.[40]

---

40 Corbin, in a May 27, 1919 letter to the national NAACP.

An arsonist destroyed the old Vallejo Methodist church, which had been sold to Kyles Temple AME Zion Church in the fall of 1919. Courtesy Vallejo Naval and Historical Museum.

During Opperman's trial in Fairfield in 1920, eyewitness Doris Larson testified she looked out her window around 5:30 AM on the morning of the blaze and saw the church in flames. At that moment, she said she witnessed Opperman "walk away very fast." After the initial fire died down, Larson said she saw

Opperman return to the church and touch a match to rubbish in the rear of the church. In an October 5, 1920 letter to the National headquarters E. C. Atkinson, Vallejo NAACP branch assistant secretary, wrote that despite Opperman's arrest, indictment and subsequent trial, "considerable prejudice was injected into the case and at times proved very humiliating. Unnecessary leniency was shown to [Opperman] and a verdict of not guilty was rendered."

VALLEJO'S NAACP VS. THE "COLORED SCHOOL"

Among the most controversial issues the Vallejo chapter faced was the Vallejo Industrial and Normal Institute, a school set up for African American boys and girls in 1911 by former Mare Island clerk Rev. Charles H. Toney. From its inception, the school at 2010 Marin Street met with resistance from Vallejo's NAACP. The school was modeled after Booker T. Washington's Tuskegee Institute in Alabama. The Vallejo NAACP viewed the school as a throwback to forced segregation that was still law in the South. For far too many Vallejo black residents, segregated schools meant unequal education no matter who was in charge.

Other black leaders, such as the Harvard-trained W.E. B. DuBois, had pushed for better education among African Americans. These leaders believed such education would allow them to compete for better pay and treatment.

Some of the issues that separated the Vallejo NAACP leadership and Toney may have boiled down to personalities, but the controversy mirrored national sentiment among black leadership who called Washington's method outdated.

At the turn of the twentieth century, Washington was considered one of the nation's most influential black leaders. Eloquent and politically savvy, Washington preached that African Americans were best served by ignoring political equality with whites. Instead, Washington believed blacks should concentrate on economic stability through vocational skills.

Many Vallejo African American leaders viewed the Toney school as a program behind the times. They were also suspicious of white Napa businessmen who lent financial support to the school. Around the same period, a similar attempt to start a "colored school" in Allensworth by its leader and founder, Colonel Allen Allensworth, was roundly criticized by state black leaders. While Colonel Allensworth was "beloved all over the world," black people were unwilling to allow separate schools for African American and white students. And because Colonel Allensworth died in 1914 as a result of an accident, the issue never came to pass in the town of Allensworth.[41]

While the Vallejo NAACP continued to express its disapproval of the school it would be close to 25 years and a lawsuit brought by the local civil rights group before the Vallejo Industrial and Normal School was finally closed.

In February 1929, Vallejo branch secretary Walter Simpson wrote a long and heartfelt letter to NAACP National Secretary James Weldon Johnson seeking assistance on how to deal with the Vallejo "colored" school. Toney, Simpson insisted, was running a "Jim Crow school."

"We have fine schools here in California ... and well-thinking Negroes don't see a need for a school like the Vallejo Industrial and Normal school," Simpson wrote.

A few months later *The Vallejo Evening Chronicle,* in a forceful editorial, called for an investigation of the school following another complaint being filed against the school by the NAACP, alleging the school was inadequate and students there had been ill-fed and improperly cared for. "The respectable, right thinking, right living section of Vallejo Negroes are the best judges as to whether this school is what it claims to be, or if it is a fake which can bring nothing but ill-repute upon the colored race and the city," the *Chronicle* noted.

By the late summer, the Vallejo NAACP filed papers in the court seeking closure of the school based on Toney's inability to run the facility. The trial not only brought out that the school was

---

41   In *The Negro Trail Blazers of California*

in poor condition and that only one student was actually enrolled at the facility but funds for the school had been mismanaged.

In a letter to the NAACP Assistant Secretary Walter White on Oct. 15, 1929, the Vallejo branch secretary proudly announced their victory in getting the Toney school closed, but lamented the enormous monetary toll the "hard fight" took on their budget. The branch had paid all but $150 of the $500 it cost to pay for the attorney and other fees.

Walter White, less than a week later, wrote Simpson congratulating the Vallejo branch on its victory. "This is so good a piece of work that I am turning it over to our Director of Publicity and asking him to send out a story on it to the press this week." Following the trial, Delilah Beasley praised the "legal ability" of Oakland attorney Lawrence Sledge, who represented the Vallejo NAACP, for the victory.[42]

Despite the judge's ruling and the resulting praise, Toney defied the order until the early 1930s, and the Vallejo Industrial and Normal School stayed open.

NAACP Organizes on a Regional Level

While Vallejo had one of the earliest NAACP branches in the state, by 1922 there were seventeen branches from Siskiyou County to San Diego.[43] In one of its most ambitious efforts, the Vallejo NAACP in 1921 organized the First Pacific Coast Conference, bringing branches from throughout the West Coast to the city. Steeped in symbolism, the two day conference held at Vallejo's Lincoln School fell on the "Great Emancipator's" February 12 birthday.

---

42   In her November 3, 1929 column *Activities Among Negroes.*
43   *The National Association for the Advancement of Colored People in California,* Gloria Harrison, (Masters thesis, Stanford University, 1949).

First

Convention

OF THE

Pacific Coast

N. A. A. C. P.

Vallejo, Cal.

February 12-13

1921

This commemorative ribbon was given out at the 1921 NAACP conference held in Vallejo at Lincoln School. Courtesy of the Library of Congress.

Every West Coast branch was invited to this anticipated event; scores of black and white people, including city officials and other leaders, attended. This conference was one of the earliest attempts to regionalize the West Coast branches. Up until that time and for years after, many West Coast branch officials felt the national office, due in part to the great distance between the West Coast and New York office, was not hearing them. It would be the 1940s before the nation's NAACP would regionalize.

At the 1921 conference, attendees hammered out bylaws for a regional organization they agreed to name "The Pacific Coast Conference of the National Association for the Advancement of (The) Colored People." The objective of the conference would be "to concentrate the moral, economic and financial forces of the local branches within the limits of the Pacific Coast states to obtain, promote and perpetuate by all lawful means democracy and justice ... for all people."

A. Wayne Amerson: The Twentieth-Century Memory Keeper

A. Wayne Amerson, 1974

In 1909, Delilah L. Beasley set out to write her story of California's black pioneers. That same year, Henry S. and Matilda Amerson and their son Alphonso Wayne moved from Beaumont, Texas to Vallejo, determined to make a new life on the West Coast. Once settled, the Amersons played a strong role in the establishment of Vallejo's black community in the twentieth century. A. Wayne Amerson (1905–1982) came to Vallejo at the age of five in 1909.[44] Sixty-four years later, he continued the story in an oral history interviews at The University of California Berkeley. His words provide an important glimpse into a forgotten era and help to connect the people and events of the nineteenth and twentieth centuries. When Amerson moved to Vallejo in 1909, John Grider was very much alive and living in the city. It's almost certain young Amerson saw Grider, who was about eighty-three in 1909. Amerson's oral history is a rare glimpse into this early North Bay life and, in fact, is the only one I have come across in my research.

Amerson vividly recalled the noisy train ride that brought him and his mother from Texas in 1909. It was the first train ride for the five-year-old. As the train pulled into its final stop at Port Costa, just across the Carquinez Straits from Vallejo, young Amerson soaked in the sounds of his new West Coast surroundings. "My mother told the story of how I stayed literally glued to the train window during the entire trip, even at night."

The real excitement was what awaited young Amerson and his family as he and his mother made their way by ferry from Port Coast to Vallejo. "I came to California and Vallejo in the good years as far as Negro children were concerned," said Amerson of those years just after the turn of the twentieth century. Amerson attended Vallejo public schools from elementary to high school and was one of the first African American children to graduate from Vallejo High School in 1922 at its location on Nebraska Street.

---

44 Interviews conducted by the Regional Oral History Office at U.C. Berkeley, 1972–1974.

Part of the reason the Amersons left Texas was because Wayne had an undisclosed physical condition that needed the best medical care the family could find. And it was in California, the Amersons believed, that medical treatment was available. Approximately one year earlier, Henry S. Amerson had moved to Vallejo to find a job and a place to live for his family. Once reunited, the Amersons moved in with L. J. and Willie Mae Williams at 915 York Street. Williams, the first black bookkeeper at Mare Island Navy Yard, was one of the most prominent African Americans in Vallejo. No doubt it was upon his recommendation that Henry Amerson, a former schoolteacher and railway clerk in his native Texas, got his job as a clerk at Mare Island.

The Amersons' new life was a good one. Within a few years, the Amersons had built a comfortable home in the 200 block of Illinois Street. While the neighborhood was largely white, there were a number of African American families in the 200, 300, and 400 blocks of Illinois Street. The families included those headed by George W. Posey, C. C. Courtney, Alex Taylor, and William Wiggins. These families were among Vallejo's most prominent African Americans.

"We as a family had and enjoyed most everything our neighbors had and did, perhaps a bit more," Amerson said, recalling family outings that included baseball games, church gatherings, and club meetings. Wayne described early years of growing up in Vallejo and attending local schools as happy days. He attended Farragut Grammar School, which was then located at the foot of Tennessee Street.

Education was important in the Amerson household that would later include two other Amerson children, Henry S. and Ralph W. By the time Wayne entered Farragut Grammar School he could read and write and knew his numbers. While Amerson was but one of a few African American children in the Vallejo school system during the early 1900s, he recalled friendly relationships with white schoolmates, and teachers who were strict but fair. They "were understanding, and merely wanted the assignments completed."

During the years leading up to World War I, two of Amerson's friends and classmates included Ivy Anderson, who in the 1930s and early 1940s would be Duke Ellington's lead singer, and Eddie "Rochester" Anderson who gained fame as Jack Benny's sidekick in the 1940s.[45]

Eddie "Rochester" Anderson was a Vallejo classmate of A. Wayne Amerson in the early 1900s.

---

45   The 1920 census notes that Ivy Anderson, 15, lived with Lewis and Bennie Jones, her uncle and aunt, in the 100 block of Denio Street in Vallejo.

Ivy Anderson lived and attended school in Vallejo in the
early twentieth century. Courtesy of Amazon.Com

The church played a vital role in the Amerson family's world.
They were among the earliest members of Second Baptist Church.
Within ten years of the Amersons' arrival, around 1917–18,
the city's growing black population had developed numerous
organizations, including the Grand United Order of Odd Fellow,
the Masons, Eastern Star, the Household of Ruth, and the Knights
of Pythias. The elder Amerson was active in most of these fraternal
organizations, serving as an officer in the Prince Hall Masons
Firma Lodge No. 27, Odd Fellows, and Knights of Pythias. He
was also a charter member of the Vallejo branch of the NAACP.

"The NAACP … was very prominent then because Vallejo
had something that very few other communities in California
had … it had a steady payroll," Amerson said. "The Negro people
of Vallejo were not wealthy, but they were compared to other
areas, well off."

A. Wayne Amerson pictured in 1933. The Bancroft Library, U.C. Berkeley.

While life was comfortable, money was tight for the Amersons. Any extra dollars were earmarked for Wayne's medical bills, the Amerson children's college education, and church.

Vallejo had an interurban electric bus that took Mare Island workers to and from work, but the family saw such transportation as a luxury. Henry Amerson, who would not buy a car until the 1940s, walked to the Mare Island ferry.

"For a long time only two or three Negro families had automobiles. We were not one of those families," Wayne explained in the oral interview.[46] Life was simple, he recalled of his early life in Vallejo. Instead of buying vegetables from the local store, the

---

46 *Northern California and Its Challenges To A Negro In The Mid-1900s*, a recorded interview of A. Wayne Amerson can be found in the Bancroft Library, University of California, Berkeley. A transcript of the interview, which was conducted through the Regional Oral History Office in 1974 can also be viewed online at *bancroft.berkeley.edu/ROHO/projects/ewge*. In addition to the oral history interview, the Bancroft Library also holds papers, periodicals, and newspaper clippings that were deposited by Amerson. Some of those items—such as articles on the Vallejo Industrial and Normal Institute, date back to 1916.

Amersons grew their own garden filled with greens, carrots, beets, string beans, and garden peas. Fruit trees were plentiful. "My mother canned some and made jelly ... and we ate well."

Wayne witnessed the burning of Kyles Temple AME Zion Church in November 1919; he was fifteen years old. The fire remained etched in Amerson's mind. Recalling the night of the fire, Amerson said his father Henry kept him out of school the day after the incident. "We...went to San Francisco where he [Henry Amerson] bought one of the finest repeating rifles I have ever seen in my life." Once back home in Vallejo, Amerson said his father looked at him and said: "Now everyone has a gun."

That incident, along with several others during this period of growing tensions, led Wayne to conclude that the tolerant Vallejo he had loved as a child was changing. Two years after graduating from high school, Wayne, who had been accepted into Prairie View College in Texas, started to notice that former schoolmates were still friendly "but their parents had begun to hold back."

Wayne would go on and complete his undergraduate and graduate degrees at Prairie View and the University of Arizona. Before returning to Vallejo in the late 1920s, Amerson taught at Langston University in Oklahoma.

In 1933 at age twenty-eight, Wayne Amerson became the first African American in state history to work for the California Relief Administrative Office. His first job with the state office was in Vallejo. Amerson, who had moved to the East Bay by the early 1940s, would eventually work and retire from the State Employment Office. He was also active in a variety of civic, political, and religious organizations such as the California Democratic Council.

Just as John Grider, George Van Blake, and Elizabeth Bundy forged new lives for themselves and others during the nineteenth century, A. Wayne Amerson and his accomplishments epitomize the pioneering spirit of the 1800s. Amerson's oral history is a rich and compelling story of not only one person's life but also serves as a window on a sizeable portion of early African American life in the United States that is often not told. Amerson was able to accomplish what people like Grider, Van Blake, and Bundy could only dream of during their lives. Amerson's life is proof that their dreams were realized.

Afterword

About two thirds into finishing this book I had what could be called a revelation: John Grider's voice, which had guided me through the first several months of my research, had quieted. I had come to rely on the Bear Flag veteran's wisdom to show me I was on the right track in my research of the early African American presence in the North Bay counties of Solano, Napa, and Sonoma.

While it may sound strange, I learned after a series of missteps and successes to trust both my guide and my instincts as I searched for information on the black men, women, and children who called the North Bay home from the 1840s to the 1920s.

"Tell my story," the voice would prompt as I dug through old, yellowed newspapers, combed through oversized deed books, and looked through old photo albums of descendents of these early pioneers.

Grider's insistent voice ebbed as I gathered more information. It was as if Grider realized he could trust me to follow through in letting the world know that he and thousands of others like him had been here.

My hope is that I can continue to call on John Grider, as I

need him. His voice is too powerful and his presence too valuable for me to stop listening.

While Grider's voice is quiet now, the researcher in me knows that his silence is only temporary. I expect at any point he will again capture my attention and whisper, "There's something else I need you to do."

Appendix A:
Other Early Families

You will find many of the African Americans who lived in the North Bay from the 1840s to 1900 listed here. I culled these names from various sources, including the U.S. Census, voter registration rolls, the 1863 Union Draft list, city directories (which often specified "colored" businesses), newspapers, books, and other publications. This is by no means a complete list. Just as today, people in the 1800s moved in and out of towns and cities to find work, to get married, and to search for other opportunities.

NAPA COUNTY

Bradford. The December 29, 1869 issue of *The Elevator* noted that Mrs. **Rebecca Bradford** was assigned by the African Methodist Episcopal Church body to serve as general missionary of the Napa AME Zion Church. The 1870 census lists Mrs. Bradford, fifty-one, as a "preacher." She was a native of Maryland.

Canner. Born in Missouri, **Paul Canner** came to California in the late 1850s. His wife, **Julia Canner** was here by 1862. They were the parents of W., Alice, Lucinda, Richard, and Matthew. Daughter Martha died September 30, 1867 according to a notice in *The Elevator*. **Elizabeth Brown** is also listed in the Canner household. They were among the earliest African American settlers to call Napa County home. The late Madeline Ontis, who provided me with a photo of Julia Canner, told me that her mother and Julia Canner were friends.[47]

Julia Canner, pictured with granddaughter Mazie Strickland, arrived in Napa County in the 1860s. Her husband Paul settled in the Napa area in the 1850s. Courtesy of the late Madeline Ontis, Napa.

Hatton. **Edward** and **Joseph Hatton** were active in African American affairs throughout the state. While the Hattons were

47   The author spoke to Madeline Ontis in July 2006.

associated with Napa County during the 1860s and 1870s, the family had a Marysville connection and may have settled there first. Edward owned a barbershop on Main Street in Napa in the mid-1800s. Edward Hatton and his son Joseph actively took part in civil rights organizations aimed at equality for African Americans throughout the mid to late 1800s. Edward and **Susan Hatton** were also the parents of **Mary** and **Clarissa.** Edward served as Napa and Vallejo agent for both *The Elevator* and *Pacific Appeal.* In 1865, Hatton gave his barber business to son Joseph and moved to Vallejo. In Vallejo, he worked as a stonecutter. That same year, Hatton served on the organizing committee for the fourth Convention of Colored Citizens of California, representing Vallejo. Edward Hatton is believed to be a founding member of Prince Hall Masons Laurel Lodge No. 6 in Marysville. He held high position within Prince Hall Masonic Grand Lodge of California. He also took up residence in San Francisco a few years later and worked in the insurance business there. At one point he owned a barbershop in Clear Lake. The Hattons' net worth was listed as $3,300 in 1870. Edward Hatton died Feb. 6, 1889 in San Francisco. Masons from throughout the state attended his funeral.

Joseph Hatton came to California in 1849 and worked as a miner. His wife, **Esther Seawell Hatton,** came to the state by ox team in 1857. The Hattons married around 1860. The Hattons, who first settled in Marysville, are on *The Negro Trail Blazers of California* list of pioneers. Joseph Hatton owned a barbershop at 128 Main Street in Napa. Joseph and Esther were parents of **Edward, Joseph, Sandy, Thomas,** and **Maud.** The Hatton family lived at Brown and Clay streets in Napa. In 1885, Joseph, who the *Napa Register* described as "the pioneer tonsorial artist, left the tools of his trade for those of the rancher." He moved his family to the hills above Dry Creek where he cleared land and built fences before settling in to his new occupation. Hatton and his family relocated to Marysville by the late 1800s or early 1900s. In 1902 and 1903, Joseph Hatton served as the Most Worshipful Grand

Master of the Prince Hall Grand Lodge of California. Joseph Hatton died on December 30, 1916 at the age of seventy-nine. Esther preceded her husband in death. She died of influenza on November 28, 1915 at the age of eighty-two. They are both buried at the Marysville City Cemetery.

Norris, Anderson. A cook aboard the U.S. warship *Cyane*, Norris deserted the ship in Sausalito, California in 1843 and made his way to Napa Valley where he joined a group of white hunters near Calistoga. He was pursued to this area by Salvador Vallejo (General Mariano Guadalupe Vallejo's brother) and killed.

Old Man Sours, Old Man Sydes, Aaron Rice, and Wash Strains. John Grider discovered these men in the early 1860s working as slaves on a ranch near Napa. Grider got word to Rev. Thomas Starr King, a prominent abolitionist and San Francisco Methodist minister, who intervened on behalf of the enslaved men.

Seawell. Matilda Seawell was born in Tennessee and was the aunt of Esther Seawell Hatton. Matilda came to Napa in bondage. Her owner was William Seawell, who was from Missouri. She was described as "a great hearted old lady and an excellent nurse." She died at the age of eighty-six in February 1880. **Abraham Seawell.** The nephew of Matilda Seawell, he too came to Napa as a slave. Born in Tennessee, he was taken to Missouri at a young age. He, his sister Esther, and their aunt Matilda came to California on an emigrant train in 1850 with a Major Seawell, brother of the family's owner William Seawell. In the early 1850s, Abraham married **Judy** who was also a slave and was brought into California by a man named Jack Woods. The Seawells had two children who died early. For a good portion of his life Abraham was a farmer and owned a large tract of land in Napa in the late 1860s and early 1870s. He died at the age of eighty in April 1894.

Sparrow. In1854, **Frederick Sparrow** was a student enrolled in the state's earliest black schools. *The Negro Trail Blazers of California* lists Frederick as attending schools in San Francisco and Sacramento in the 1850s. In 1870, he became one of the first African Americans to register to vote in the Bay Area following the ratification of the Fifteenth Amendment. On June 7, 1865, Frederick and **Alice Scott** were married by the Rev. J. J. Hubbard in the Sacramento home of the bride's mother. Sparrow was a native of Missouri, while Alice hailed from North Carolina. In 1870 at the age of twenty-seven, he owned a barbershop at 52 Main Street in Napa. They were the parents of **Nellie** and **Ida May.** The Sparrows' youngest son, ten-month-old **Sherlock**, died in November 1869 according to a notice in *The Elevator.* The 1870 census lists grandmother Nellie in the Sparrow household. Sparrow's wife Alice may have died in the early or mid-1870s. A Feb. 3, 1877 newspaper announcement proclaimed he had married **Jennie B. Hall** in Napa. By 1880 the census only lists Nellie Sparrow, eighty-four, and her twelve-year-old granddaughter as living in Napa.

Stewart. **Cas (Charles) Stewart** was a native of Pennsylvania. The 1860 census noted that Stewart owned a "dance house." By the 1880 census it listed him as a "hotel keeper." He was married to **Cecelia,** who is listed as white.

Stringer. **Elizabeth Stringer** was born in Africa. The 1870 census records she was married to **Harry.**

Clear Lake

Ernestine (no last name given). She was sixteen and is listed as servant in the 1860 census in the household of James E. Allen, a Kentucky-born white farmer and his family.

Jackson, William. Born in Bermuda, the 1860 census lists him as a carpenter.

Taylor, Nathaniel and *Catherine.* He was a laborer.

<u>Hot Springs</u>

Hutton, M. Lois. Born in California, the 1900 census lists her as a nurse at the St. Helena Sanitarium.

Taylor, Catherine. She was born in Massachusetts and is listed in the 1860 census.

Williams, Alonso. He was born in New York and is listed in the 1860 census.

<u>Knox</u>

Priceall (maybe Pearsall), *Charles.* Born in California, his age is recorded as thirty-four years old in 1900.

<u>Monticello</u>

Cage. Brothers **Robert W.** and **John D. Cage,** who were listed as mulattoes, were born in California. According to the census, they lived in Monticello in 1880. Under occupation, the census records the brothers were "working on house."

Panyer, Thomas. According to the 1880 census, Panyer was twenty-seven, born in California, and worked as a teamster.

<u>St. Helena</u>

McInnis, Aloussa. He was a servant.

<u>Yountville</u>

Cartright, H.C. Born in Kentucky, he is listed in the 1860 census.

Grigsby. The 1860 census first lists **Hiram Grigsby** as thirty years old. He worked as a "white washer." By 1870, he was a farmer and was married to **Annie**. In an "Information Wanted" notice in *The Elevator* in 1872, Hiram Bigsby (no doubt a misspelling) sought "information on his wife, **Patsy Stokes,** or of his children, **Margaret, Amos, and Hiram**. When last heard from, they were residing in Pulaski County, Missouri. They can hear from their father and husband, and receive substantial aid and comfort by addressing P. A. Bell, Ed. Elevator, or William Veasey St. Helena, Napa. Co., Cal 10 a.m. to 6 p.m." Hiram and Annie are listed in the 1880 census.

Johnson, Ann. The 1860 census lists her birthplace as New York, and her profession as a chambermaid.

Solano County

Benicia

Brown, Peter. Listed as seventy years old in the 1860 census, he worked as a laborer. He listed $1,000 in personal property. A death notice published in *The Elevator* in 1868 said Brown died in Benicia at the age of ninety. The notice said Brown, a native of Dinwiddie County, Virginia, came to California from Canada.

Bundy, Elizabeth. Listed as fifty-five years old in the 1860 census, she was born around 1805 in Clay, Kentucky. Bundy purchased her home on "E" street near First Street in Benicia in 1865. She worked as a cook for Bernard C. Whitman, a prominent Benicia attorney. She died on April 1, 1881.

Cason. **Joseph H. Cason** served as an agent for *The Elevator* (1870). A native of Virginia, Cason was a barber by trade. In 1867, he owned a barbershop on First Street. In April 1869, he and **Cornelia** were married in Benicia by the **Rev. J. Lloyd Breck**, principal of St. Augustine's Episcopal College. *The Elevator* covered the wedding. Also in the Cason household in 1870 was **Virginia Steele,** age seven. By 1880, the Casons had moved to San Francisco where Joseph continued to work as a barber. Cornelia was listed as a "theater dresser."

Clanton. Born in Virginia, **Simon P. Clanton** was a barber during the 1860s. He was a frequent contributor to *The Pacific Appeal* and *The Elevator* newspapers, writing on subjects related to slavery and politics. In April 1862, he was appointed Benicia agent for *The Pacific Appeal.* For a number of years he served as an agent to *The Elevator.* His wife, **S. J. Clanton**, was born in Ohio. Their children included **E. B., A. H.** and **Eliza Clanton.** In 1863, Clanton was on a committee that planned a Grand Jubilee to mark President Abraham Lincoln's signing of the Emancipation Proclamation. In 1865, Clanton presided over a committee to choose a Solano County delegate for the Convention of Colored Citizens that was held October 25–27 of that year. The committee, co chaired by W. H. Miller, chose N. E. Speights as Solano delegate.

Jackson, Catherine. Born in Kentucky, the 1870 census lists her as fifty-five. She purchased her home in Benicia in the early 1860s. She was the mother of **Mary Lane,** another longtime Benicia resident. Catherine Jackson was known as "Aunt Kitty" throughout Benicia. In 1866, she placed an ad in *The Elevator* in search of her children, who'd been left behind in Missouri.

Catherine Jackson's 1866 "Information Wanted" notice. It reads: "Information Wanted: Of the following persons: Mary Ann Ringo, America and Henry Thompson, of Liberty City, Clay County, Missouri; also of Susannah and Eleanor Darby, who resided near Liberty, and Harrison Kane of Platte City, Missouri. Any information of the above parties will be gladly received by this mother, Catherine Jackson, of Benicia. She came to California from Missouri, with Mr. Marsh, in 1852. The "Nationalist of Mobile, and "Tennesseean" of Nashville, will publish the above one month and send bill to the office of this paper. We will remit immediately on receipt of bills.

Lane, Mary (Ringo). She came to California in the 1870s. She lived with her son Dorsey on the southwest corner of I and Second Street, Benicia. In *The Negro Trail Blazers of California*, author Delilah L. Beasley interviewed Mary Lane in the early 1900s. At the time of the interview, Lane was a resident of the Home for Aged and Infirm Colored People in Oakland. She told Beasley her mother (Catherine Jackson) first came to California in 1852. Mary and a brother came from Missouri in the 1870s to join their mother in California. (See Information Wanted advertisement.) When Lane died in March 1937, Rev. William M. Dixon of the Second Baptist Church conducted her funeral. Several prominent Vallejo residents served as pallbearers, including A. J. Smith, J.

M. Ward, W. Thomas, George W. Posey, E. Russell, and Jock R. Taylor.

McAfee, Joseph. One of seven African American Bear Flag Party veterans, McAfee lived in Benicia until the 1860s. By 1870, the census listed McAfee as living in Santa Cruz where he operated a couple of businesses, including an oyster house across from the Pacific Ocean. A staunch supporter of African American suffrage, McAfee was a speaker at a Watsonville event marking the passage of the Fifteenth Amendment in 1870. McAfee died at the age of fifty-seven on May 23, 1878.

Ross. Born in Missouri, **Dorsey Ross** was the son of Mary Lane. He and his wife **Mary** were long time residents of Benicia. For many years he worked as a janitor at the Bank of Benicia. He was a member of Prince Hall Masons Firma Lodge No. 27, Vallejo. To celebrate his mother's one-hundredth birthday in 1930, Ross hosted a party at the Home for Aged and Infirm Colored People, the Oakland nursing home where Mary Lane stayed the last years of her life. Family, friends, and residents of the home attended the party.

Townsend, Abigail. In a February 18, 1870 notice in *The Elevator*, "Miss Abigail Townsend came to California in 1858 and went to reside near Benicia. If she will address a letter to P.A. Bell, editor, Elevator, San Francisco, she will learn something to her advantage."

Elmira and Rio Vista

Stepp. Born in Kentucky, **Mattie Stepp** (listed in the 1900 census) had four children: **Willie, Lula, Cecil,** and **Freddie.**

Turner, Virgil. Born in California, this forty-year-old was a day laborer in 1900.

Fairfield

Briscoe, Erastus. A barber by trade, the thirty-nine-year-old Briscoe was born in Virginia and is listed in the 1860 census. He owned four hundred dollars in real estate and property. In 1863, Briscoe served as the Suisun representative on a committee that planned a Grand Jubilee to mark President Abraham Lincoln's signing of the Emancipation Proclamation.

Craig, Silas. Born in Kentucky, the 1860 census noted he had $825 in real estate and personal property. He is also listed as living in Fairfield in the 1880 census.

Jones. A wheelwright, **Clayton Jones** owned a carriage shop in Fairfield in the 1860s. The 1870 census lists him as thirty years old. He hailed from Missouri. In the late 1860s, he hosted visitors from *The Elevator* who came to Fairfield to write about the area. An 1874 Solano County directory listed Jones as working as a carpenter. The Jones family included his wife, **Catherine,** and daughter, **Ann Elizabeth.** Also in the Jones household was **Margaret Conerway,** who was listed as "grandmother."

Towns, William. Longtime agent for *The Elevator,* he served as a steward on a Bay Area steamer. Towns was a third sergeant in the San Francisco-based Brannan Guards, a black volunteer military drill company. He is listed on *The Negro Trail Blazers of California* pioneer list.

Silveyville (Dixon)

Gilliard, J. E. M. A lecturer and writer, he lived in Silveyville for a short period during the 1860s. Often referred to as Professor Gilliard in *The Elevator,* he was born in New York. He served as an agent and writer for the San Francisco-based newspaper. Gilliard traveled extensively throughout Northern California and adjoining states during the late 1860s and early 1870s collecting subscriptions and stories for *The Elevator.* In June 1869, Gilliard lectured in Vallejo, Fairfield, and Napa on issues regarding the equal treatment of African Americans. By 1873, Gilliard moved back east where he continued to write and lecture.

Suisun

Craven. **Oscar Craven** was a cook and in the 1874 Solano County Directory, he was listed as working at Littrell's Restaurant. He and his wife, Mary, were the parents of **Joseph, Caroline,** and **Oscar.** The elder Craven is listed in the 1860, 1870, 1880, and 1900 censuses.

Gibson, Charles H. In 1869, the former Benicia resident now living in Suisun City, along with Joseph H. Cason, was on the committee planning a Grand Picnic that was held in San Francisco on June 8. The committee promised that the picnic would be "the grandest affair of the season." The picnic was held under the auspices of the Union Club and held at the City Gardens.

Smith. **Margaret Smith,** wife of **William M. Smith,** was a hairdresser who owned a salon on Main Street. She advertised in *The Elevator* in 1868. On July 3, 1868 she gave birth to a daughter (no name given).

Stewart, William H. He owned a combination restaurant, lodging house, barbershop, and bathing saloon "where only the best are employed." Stewart advertised in *The Elevator* on May 1, 1868.

Vacaville

Baker, Squire. Missouri-born, he worked as a "hostler" in local livery stable. He registered to vote in 1896.

Squire Baker of Vacaville registered to vote in the 1890s.
Courtesy the Vacaville Heritage Council.

Jeans, Daniel. Born in Missouri, he worked as a laborer. He is listed in the 1860 census. The 1870 census noted that he had moved to the Russian River area in Sonoma.

Moore, John. Born in Ohio, the 1860 census lists nineteen-year-old Moore as working for W. Cantelow.

Brunson. In his last will and testament published in *The Elevator* on December 4, 1868, **Lewis Brunson** left his entire estate, including a farm, to his wife **Eliza Jane** on the condition she would not remarry. If she remarried, only one third of the estate would be hers, with the remaining two thirds going to his sister **Mary Jane George** and his brother, **Samuel Brunson**. In his will, which was drawn up by a San Francisco attorney, Benson left all claims to his father's property in Salem County, New Jersey to his brother Samuel. Although Lewis Brunson lived in Vallejo, he owned property back east; his last will said his remaining property in Middletown, New Jersey was to be divided between his niece and wife.

Clark, John Balfour. A barber by trade, he was born in the West Indies. He became a naturalized citizen in the 1880s. He was registered to vote in Vallejo in 1896.

Clarke. Born in England, **Simon P. Clarke** was in the household of John Richards in Santa Rosa in the 1860 census. By 1870, Clarke lived in Vallejo. His family included wife **Laura**, who was born in New York, and children, **Lillie**, **Laura**, **John**, and **Simon**. All the Clarke children were born in California. The Clarke family is listed in the 1870 and 1880 censuses. Clarke served as conductor of the Pacific Brass Band. On Feb. 20, 1868, he conducted the band at a Grand Promenade Concert held at Dashaway Hall on Post Street in San Francisco. In the 1870s, Clarke owned a barbershop on Sacramento Street in Vallejo. The Clarkes had moved their business to Georgia Street by the late 1870s. Simon and Laura operated their barber and hairdressing salon for more than twenty-five years. He had a half-page ad in Vallejo city directory in 1870. Clarke, a member of Prince Hall Masons Victoria Lodge No. 3 was a prominent in California Masonic affairs. He was a Royal Arch Mason and served as a grand secretary of the Prince Hall Masons Grand Lodge of California in 1869.

Dixon. A barber by trade, **Wilson Dixon** owned a barbershop at the corner of Santa Clara and Georgia streets in Vallejo in the 1860s and 1870s. He and his wife, **Jane,** lived on Santa Clara near Capitol Street. The Dixons, according to the 1870 census, had four children: **Jane, Clara, Johanna,** and **Clay.** By 1880, the census lists two additional Dixon children, **Katty** and **Walter.** The children were enrolled in the local school system. Dixon played a prominent role in early statewide efforts seeking equal education rights for black children.

Grove. **Thomas Moore Grove** was born in Jamaica. Before his arrival in California, Grove served as the San Antonio, Texas agent for *The Pacific Appeal.* He owned a restaurant at 63 Georgia Street (near the wharf) from the late 1860s through the 1870s. Grove (sometimes identified as Groves) held high positions in Prince Hall Masons of California in the 1880s. In 1880, Grove was the state Lodge's Grand Pursuivant. He registered to vote with John Grider in the 1880s and 1890s. The 1897 Vallejo city directory listed Grove, whose wife was named Martha, as a janitor. He died in Vallejo in 1900.

Hawkins. Born in New York, **George W. Hawkins** is associated with Napa and Vallejo. His family included wife, **Sarah** (born in North Carolina), and children, **Mallissa** and **Lilla,** who were born in California. The family had seven hundred dollars in real estate and property. On May 18, 1868, *The Elevator* newspaper reported that a fire swept through downtown Vallejo "destroying some of the finest buildings in the city." Hawkins' hairdressing salon on Georgia Street was among those that went up in flame. The 1870 Vallejo city directory listed Hawkins as a barber at the Carquinez Hotel in South Vallejo.

Silva. Freeborn, **Joseph and Louisa Silva** worked for Dr. Elish Ely. They are listed in the 1850 census.

Graham, Jacob. The 1860 Sonoma County census listed sixteen-year-old **Jacob Graham's** occupation as "slave." What became of Jacob is still unknown.

Petaluma

Barnes. **Lewis Barnes** was born in Maryland, his wife, **Margaret (Aunt Peggy),** was born in Virginia. They are listed in the 1860 census. Mrs. Barnes is listed on *The Negro Trail Blazers of California* pioneer list. The Barnes purchased their property on the north side of F Street in 1861. Lewis died in January 1871, while Peggy Barnes died in July 1890. Her grave marker has been found at Cypress Hill though no mark has been located for her husband.

Clark, Ellen. She is on *The Negro Trail Blazers of California* pioneer list. She came from Polk County, Missouri in 1849 by ox team. "There were sixty souls in the party and 2000 head of cattle. The party located at Honey Lake Valley, hence to Santa Rosa, hence to Petaluma, where Mrs. Clark became the wife of **Mr. Piper.**"

Holmes. **Henry Holmes** was born in Virginia around 1832; **Sara A. Holmes** was born in Pennsylvania around 1845. They married in Quincy, Illinois, on March 25, 1865. He worked as a carpet weaver. Henry saw service in the Civil War, serving in the 13th US Colored Troops Heavy Artillery from March to November 1865. After settling in California, he and Sara purchased a home from Robert Looney on May 8, 1875. The home was located at 28 Liberty Street. Henry and Sarah purchased three lots in 1887. By 1895, a city directory recorded a Henry Holmes on Fair Street between English and Bassett streets. Sara died on February 21,

1904 and Henry died on November 30, 1906. At the time of his death, Henry bequeathed his house on Liberty Street to the First Baptist Church to be used as the parsonage (renamed the Holmes Memorial Parsonage). From 1908 to 1913 the **Rev. Robert N. Lynch** of the First Baptist Church and his family lived in the Holmes parsonage.

Johnson. **Ann J. Johnson** was born in Missouri. She is listed as "keeping house" in the 1880 census. She was the mother of **Nancy**, twenty-one, **George**, twelve, and nine-year-old **Belle** Johnson. George was listed "at school." All the children were born in California.

Johnson. **Thomas Johnson** was born in Virginia and worked as a laborer. **Julianna Johnson** was born in South Carolina. The Johnsons had three children: Gracie, R. B., Rosa Ann, and George, all born by 1868. Their personal property was valued at three hundred dollars. Thomas was a trustee of the Union African Methodist Episcopal. He died in Sonoma County on November 16, 1879 and is believed to be buried at Cypress Hill. The Johnsons are listed in the 1870 census.

McFarland. Born in Tennessee, **Alex McFarland** worked as a laborer. His wife, **Melvina,** was born in Florida. The McFarlands lived at 411 Fifth Street. The house may have been the site of the Petaluma "colored school." The 1880 census said the couple had one daughter, **Eliza,** who was twelve years old and listed as "at school." Eliza was born in California. An obituary in 1886 noted that Alexander was born into slavery and was a slave when he arrived in California in the 1850s. Melvina died in 1900.

Miller. New Jersey native **George W. Miller** is listed in both the 1860 and 1870 census. He and his wife **Catherine**, a native of Washington DC, were the parents of four children, **Elizabeth**, **Edward**, **Mary**, and **Theodore**. In April 1862, he was appointed

Petaluma agent for *The Pacific Appeal*. Miller was active on a statewide committee that championed educational rights for African American children. In *The Elevator*, Miller is referred to as Captain G. W. Miller, in reference to his position in the Colfax Guard, a military marching unit made up of African American men. The 1870 census lists four-year-old **Richard Robinson** in the Miller household.

Smith. **Irwin C. Smith** was born in North Carolina, while his wife, **Elizabeth,** hailed from Georgia. He was a laborer. They lived next door to the McFarlands. The Smiths are listed in the 1870 census.

Analy (Sebastopol)

Crooks, Robert. A survivor of the ill-fated Donner Party, he came to Sonoma County in 1846. Born in Missouri, he worked as a laborer and is listed in the 1880 census. In 1898, Crooks was one of twenty-seven Sonoma County pioneers who were recognized as being in California before gold was discovered in January of 1848. The *Santa Rosa Press Democrat*, in an article that appeared in the paper on December 15, 1897, noted that Crooks and the other Sonoma County pioneers would be feted at a Jubilee Celebration in San Francisco in January 1898. Crooks died on May 17, 1904. The day after his death, *The San Francisco Call* ran a short article:

Donner Party Survivor Dies

Robert Crooks, a negro who was one of the survivors of the Donner party, passed away this afternoon at the County hospital, where he had been spending his remaining days. Crooks was a native of Missouri, aged 76 years, and death was due to heart failure. When the Donner party departed from their Eastern home for California, Crooks was a servant in the family of that name and elected to come with the trip.

Santa Rosa

Richards. **John Richards** was a prominent businessman who owned several businesses in Santa Rosa, Ukiah, and Lakeport. Following emancipation, Richards' home became a refuge for freed slaves seeking new lives in California. An avid community leader, Richards lent financial support to a school for African American children in the 1860s. He and his wife **Philena** had two children, **Ella** and **Frank.** John Richards served as an agent for *The Elevator*. On July 31, 1867, at a convention of the Phoenixonian Institute in San Jose, Richards was appointed vice-president of the institute's nominating committee. The institute, which was founded on December 22, 1863, organized "for the religious, moral and political improvement of the colored people of the state of California."

Johnson, Amos. Born in the West Indies, he served as a teacher at the Santa Rosa school for African American children during the 1860s. He was a member of the United Sons of Friendship, serving as secretary to the Sacramento-based organization. *(The Elevator, Aug. 18, 1869)*

Davidson (Davison). **Henry W. Davidson** was born in Savannah, Georgia on August 10, 1810. Davidson was the son of a Jamaican mother and an English father. At thirteen, he left Georgia for New York where he would eventually become associated with the missionaries of the well-known Oberlin College. When he was twenty-one, Davidson was sent to Jamaica to teach for several years and became a member of the London Missionary Society. In ensuing years, Davidson became head steward of the Panama railroad, which provided transportation for the thousands of gold seekers heading to California who had to cross the Isthmus of Panama. In the mid-1800s, Davidson would also become an associate of William Walker, an adventurer and soldier of fortune who attempted to conquer several Latin American countries. Walker eventually proclaimed himself President of Nicaragua.

By 1870, Davidson was in the North Bay Area, first living in Petaluma and then relocating to Santa Rosa, where he earned a living as a boot black. He died an indigent on February 16, 1899.

Lewis, Solomon. He was born in Illinois.

Potter. A native of Louisiana, the 1880 census records **Edmond P. Potter** as a farmer. He died in January 1908. An article in the *San Francisco Call* on January 8, 1908 read:

Stands to Attention and Band Plays as Funeral Train of "Uncle Potter" passes

Yesterday afternoon while the Woodmen of the World were returning from the local cemetery after having attended the annual memorial exercises, they met the funeral cortege of the late "Uncle Potter," the colored pioneer.

The band boys and members of the drill team formed lines on either side of the street, and with the drill axes presented and the band playing "Old Folks at Home" and "Nearer My God To Thee," they stood while the cortege passed.

"Uncle Potter" died here at the age of 91 years and was one of the best known and most highly respected men in the community, and his passing caused general sorrow in the entire community.

Healdsburg

Dennison. According to the 1860 census, **A. B. Dennison** was a barber. He was married to **Rebecca.** In the Dennison household were **Marcus A. Bell**, barber, and **Joseph P. Taylor.**

Harper, William H. He was born in Maryland and is listed in the 1860 census.

Jamison, Savannah. Born in Mississippi, she was thirteen in 1880. She was listed as a servant in the household of lawyer Albert Shannon. No family is listed for Savannah.

Sonoma

Clark, William E. Born in Kentucky, the 1900 census listed Clark, twenty-two, as living in the California Home for the Care and Training of Feeble-Minded Children. Also at the facility was **Jessie Dan**, who was twenty.

Howell, Charles. He was born in Virginia. Married to Martha, the 1860 census records that the couple had three children. The elder Howell is also listed in the 1870 census.

Jackson, Maria. As part of a "ladies plan," she helped raise money for *The Elevator* during the 1860s. The March 27, 1868 newspaper reports she donated $2.50 to the newspaper to help keep it operating.

Shanklin, Robert. The 1870 census listed Shanklin as fifty-three years old. He was born in Delaware.

Forestville

Smith, Sarah. She was born in California and worked as a servant.

Washington

Dunlap, Auriller. Born in California, the 1900 census records she was twenty-six years old.

Morris, Edward. Born in Kentucky, he is listed as a farmer in the 1860 census.

<u>Bodega</u>

Ali, Henry. The 1870 census records he was born in "East India." His occupation was listed as a laborer.

McClure, S. Born in Missouri, the 1870 census lists him as working as a cook.

Sloan, C. F. Born in Pennsylvania, he was a barber. He was sixty-three years old in 1880.

<u>Mendocino</u>

Howell. **Charles Howell** was born in Virginia. The 1870 census records his age as seventy-five. In his household was **Anne,** thirteen, who was born in California.

Tabb, Elizabeth E. Born in California, she was a servant.

Tombs. **Ellen Tombs** was born in Missouri. A domestic servant, she was the mother of **Minnie, Taylor, Edward, Amanda,** and **Sarah Tombs.** In 1870, they were in the household of William H. Tombs, a white farmer.

Williams, Mary A. She was born in Virginia.

<u>Russian River</u>

Harris, Samuel. He was born in Tennessee. He was a servant.

Hewlet, Alex. The 1870 census records this twenty-one-year-old was born in Tennessee.

<u>Cloverdale</u>

Myers, Charles. Born in New York, this eighteen-year-old worked as a dishwasher for a West Street business, according to the 1870 census.

Appendix B:
Gravestones Mark the Final Resting Place of Many Early North Bay African American

Early African American residents who called the North Bay home are buried in cemeteries throughout area towns and cities including Vallejo, Benicia, Napa, and Santa Rosa. While many of the tombstones marking their graves are no longer evident, many still stand.

Benicia City Cemetery
Mary Ann (Ringo) Lane is buried in Benicia City Cemetery. In October 2004, the Benicia Historical Society dedicated and placed a headstone on the unmarked grave of Mary Lane. She is buried next to her mother Catherine Jackson, who died in 1882, as well as Elizabeth Bundy, who died in 1881. Bundy and Jackson may have been related. They may have come to California at the same time sometime in the 1850s.

Carquinez Cemetery – Vallejo
In Vallejo, George and Elizabeth Van Blake, along with their son William, are buried at Carquinez Cemetery on Benicia Road. George died in 1917. Elizabeth died in 1918. Their son died in 1892 at the age of 29. There are no tombstones to mark their graves.

Simon Clarke died on November 3, 1883. His wife Laura died October 28, 1909. She was sixty-four years old. They are both buried at Carquinez Cemetery.

Cypress Hill Cemetery – Petaluma
Peggy Barnes, a longtime resident of Petaluma, died in 1890 and is buried in Cypress Hill Cemetery in Petaluma. No tombstone has been located for her husband Lewis.

Henry Holmes and his wife Sara are buried side by side in the Cypress Hill Cemetery in Petaluma. While there is a marker on his grave showing he died in 1906, his wife's grave is not marked, though it is known she died two years before her husband.

The gravestone of Henry Holmes, an African American veteran of the Civil War. Holmes, a longtime resident of Petaluma owned a number of properties in the area. Courtesy of Katherine Rinehart, Sonoma County Library.

Petaluma residents Alexander and Melvina McFarland came to California in the 1850s. Alexander died in 1886, while Melvina died in 1900. They are buried in Cypress Hill Cemetery.

Headstone of Melvina McFarland. Courtesy, Katherine Rinehart, Sonoma County Library.

Headstone of Alexander McFarland. Courtesy Katherine Rinehart, Solano County Library.

Mare Island Cemetery

A number of African American seamen are buried at the Mare Island Cemetery. William Hubbard, a native of Bermuda who died at the navy yard in 1876, is buried here.

J. H. McShin, a mess attendant aboard the *USS Solace*, died in 1902 and is buried at Mare Island Cemetery.

John William Marshall, a mess attendant, second class was stationed at Mare Island in the early 1900s. He died of tuberculosis on October 19, 1904 and is buried at Mare Island. He was born in Chetaw, South Carolina

Santa Rosa Rural Cemetery

When John Richards, the well-known and wealthy businessman, died in Santa Rosa in April 1879, hundreds of people from throughout the Bay Area attended his funeral. His prominence and wealth is reflected in the impressive tombstone that marks both his and his wife Philena's grave. Hs wife died about a year later.

The brass plaque on John and Philena Richards' tombstone.
Courtesy of Santa Rosa Rural Cemetery.

The tombstone of John and Philena Richards is in the Rural Cemetery in Santa Rosa. Courtesy of Santa Rosa Rural Cemetery.

Henry W. Davidson, August 12, 1810–February 16, 1899, was first buried in a Potter's Field following his death. It had been known that Davidson had wanted to be buried next to his wife, Jane, in the Santa Rosa Rural Cemetery. *The Press Democrat* came forward and paid the difference in cost and Davidson was laid to rest in the cemetery's Main Circle. There is no marker on the grave site.

Suisun-Fairfield Cemetery – Fairfield

John Grider, Vallejo pioneer and Bear Flag veteran is buried at the Suisun-Fairfield Cemetery in Fairfield. Grider, who died on December 23, 1924, is buried in a common grave with the remains of other deceased patients of the Solano County Hospital.

This is one of four small gravestones marking the burial site of John Grider at the Suisun-Fairfield Cemetery in Fairfield. Photo: Clarence Payne.

Adam Willis is buried in the Odd Fellows section of the Suisun-Fairfield Cemetery on Union Street in Fairfield. Willis died on November 20, 1902 at the age of seventy-six. Known far and wide in his community, "the fact that so large a number attended the funeral was evident of the esteem in which he was held," his obituary read. Buried next to him is his grandniece Laura who died in 1887 at the age of sixteen.

Tulocay Cemetery – Napa

Mary Ellen Pleasant, often called the Mother of Civil Rights in California, is buried in Tulocay Cemetery, Napa. Pleasant, who died on January 4, 1904, owned a share in a ranch near Napa. Days before her death, Pleasant made arrangements with her attorney to be laid to rest in a plot in Napa owned by her friend, J. L. Sherwood. Pleasant was a leading figure in nineteenth century California.[48] A shrewd businesswoman, she raised money to help African American in their quest for equal rights. In 1866, Pleasant along with two other black women, were forced off a San Francisco streetcar. Pleasants sued the streetcar company and won. Her lawsuit, *Pleasant v. North Beach & Mission Railroad Company*, outlawed segregation in the city's public conveyances. Her grave marker reads: "Mary Ellen Pleasant, mother of civil rights in California, 1812–1904, she was a friend of John Brown, San Francisco Negro Historical and Cultural Society Memorial." The small brass plaque in the upper right corner reads: "Mammy Pleasant, in memory ... honors one of the most remarkable, unique women of early San Francisco history. Dedicated February 4, 1978, Mammy Pleasant Benevolent Society, of Sam Brannen Chapter No. 1004, E Clampus Vitus."

Mary Ellen Pleasant, often referred to as the Mother of Civil Rights in early California, is buried in Tulocay Cemetery in Napa.

48 *San Francisco Call*, January 12, 1904.

Appendix C:
Students Enrolled in the Vallejo
Industrial and Normal School, 1916

In a December 1916 report to the Vallejo Industrial and Normal Institute Board of Directors, Charles H. Toney, principal of the school for African Americans, outlined an ambitious plan for expansion of the Vallejo Industrial and Normal School.

"Vigorous efforts are being made to add a farm of fifty acres to the plant to teach the pupils how to work with their hands and to give them proper exercise in the pure air," Toney reported to the board.

The school—now the site of St. John Missionary Baptist Church—was established five years earlier. The school, modeled after those set up by Booker T. Washington, was primarily geared to training young people as domestic workers.

"In the Domestic Science Department the work is progressing nicely," Toney explained. "The school has not been able to supply the demands for cooks and maids trained here."

The school also boasted an agricultural department, which in 1916 Toney reported, was "progressing very well. The potatoes and bean crops as well as other varieties of vegetables such as are grown in this section of the state were very good this year."

During 1916 Toney said horses and delivery wagons purchased "have added much to the convenience of the school ... and reduced the cost of supplies needed for the school."

While the Vallejo NAACP would years later lead an effort to close down the school—they claimed the school had only one student and was badly managed—Toney's 1916 report to the board of directors painted an impressive picture of the facility. Students enrolled at the school during 1916 included:

El Cerrito:
Dorsie L. Jones
Katherine Harris
Bennie Northern
Nancy L. Crane
Fleeta Rosemond
Boaz Rosemond
Imperial:
Alma Franklin
Half Moon Bay:
Ella May Clarke
Fresno:
Lottie Lucille Brown
Madera:
Emma L. Beaman
Vallejo:
Amelia Davis
Elizabeth Bost
Alberta Hatcher
Oakland:
Mildred Miller
Lorraine and Cecelia Smith
Trinidad, Colorado:
Murdo Blackwood

Appendix D:
Prince Hall Masons, Firma Lodge No. 27 Membership List, 1918

Detail from Firma Lodge No. 27, Vallejo letterhead used in the 1920s.
Courtesy of Prince Hall F&AM, Firma Lodge No. 27, Vallejo.

Following is a list of many of the early members of Prince Hall Masons Firma Lodge No. 27 from 1918 to 1925. Many of these men were also members of the Spanish-American Veterans group, the Grand United Order of Odd Fellows and the Knights of Pythias.

L. J. (Louis James) Williams – Lodge organizer
Alex Taylor – Lodge organizer
James E. Berry – Lodge organizer
M. D. Akers
B. A. Alexander
E. Alley
Dennis Alves

Henry S. Amerson
B. J. Bailey
D. E. Barnes
Paul Benton
Curtis Bigsby
Charles Blackwood
T. W. Boyden
B. Brown
R. Brown
S. C. Brown
William H. Campbell
Cullen D. Cannon
L. S. Cannon
A. B. Caviel
A. L. Cownings
Scipio Chance
C. C. Courtney
P. Coleman
J. H. Dunn
S. E. Edwards
L. P. Findley
William Fleming
Guy Flowers
William J. Fryson
William Garrett
Frank Geary
Charley A. Gomez
W. E. Greene
E. Hall
J. D. Harris
H. L. Hatcher
Daniel Hause
R. D. Higginbotham
Marion Hill
S. House

Fred Houston
William Hughes
Howard Jackson
J. W. Jones
Louis Jones
Hayes (Haze) Johnson
T. S. Johnson
Brooks Johnston
John W. Johnson Sr.
John W. Johnson Jr.
John L. Malone
William Marshall
Prince Mattis
William A. McDowell
Clark McGee
Garrett McGee
E. D. Medallo
R. Mitchell
Alexander Morrow
E. U. Moore
J. W. Mosby
James Owens
J. J. Nelson
W. Nelson
A. J. Nottage
Lewis Peace
G. W. Pitts
R. C. Poole
George W. Posey
George Rice
Ed Roach
Moses Robinson
Robert Robinson
Rodriguez
H. H. Rollins

Salmon
Charles Self
Frank Scales
O. M. Scruggs
Richard H. Simpkins
L.J. Smith
Sylvester Spriggs
E. A. Stepp
George A. Stubbs
B. W. Taylor
Jock R. Taylor
C. H. Tinsley
J. C. Turner
R. Vance
John Watts
S. D. Westmoreland
G. W. White
L. A. White
William Wiggans
Peter Williams
Norman Woodall
William Woods
William C. Wyne

Worshipful Masters
1919 - L. J. Williams
1920 - Alex Taylor
1921 - L. J. Williams
1922 - Sylvester Spriggs
1923 - W. C. Wyne
1924 - E. U. Moore
1925 - H. S. Amerson

Appendix E:
NAACP Vallejo Branch Original
Membership List, 1917

Seventy-one area residents, mostly all Vallejoans, answered the call to join the local branch of the National Association for the Advancement of Colored People (NAACP) when the civil rights group organized in July 1918. The following list was sent to the NAACP's New York headquarters. Members, who paid $1 dues, included Vallejo's most prominent residents. While membership came largely from Vallejo, the civil rights organization had members from Benicia, Martinez, and San Francisco, including McCant Stewart, a prominent lawyer who practiced in San Francisco.

D. G. Corbin
Mrs. J.L. Malone
Fred D. Clopton
Jas. M. Owens
T. J. Anderson
H. S. Anderson

Mrs. Emma Buckner
A. B. Caviel
Mrs. D. C. Corbin
Mrs. F. D. Clopton
Mrs. F. Crowley
A. W. Coleman
G. L. Churchill
C. C. Courtney
E. Courtney
Mrs. E. Copeland
Mrs. M. L. Dixon
Mrs. F. Geary
F. Geary
Mrs. E. V. Hall
Fred Houston
G. W. Hixon
D. M. Johnson
F. M. Johnson
W. Johnson
C. Jones
L. Lockwood
L. Jones
Mrs. L.H. Langley
Frank Wilner
G. A. Miller
E. W. Moore
J. L. Malone
Mrs. E. W. Moore
C. (Clarke) McGee
C. C. Miller
Mrs. C. C. Miller
Mrs. James Owens
G. W. Posey
Mrs. G.W. Posey
L. Ramson

S. Spriggs
Mrs. S. Spriggs
Mrs. L.J. Smith
Albert Smith
I. Maxwell
McCant Stewart (Vallejo attorney)
Mrs. S. Sneed
Alex Taylor
J. R. Taylor
M. Toney
C. B. Toney
W. Tingle
Leon Tingle
W. Towns
E. M. Thomas
Mrs. L. J. Williams
L. J. Williams
Mrs. W. H. Wiggins
C. L. West
W. Whitney
Vassa Wysinger
Mrs. G. Ross
Mrs. W. E. Green
W. H. Garrett
J. H. Thomas
W. Watkins
M. Robinson
W. C. Wyne

Appendix F:
Slavery in the North Bay

While on paper California may have been a free state when it was admitted into the union in 1850, for more than a thousand African Americans—including scores who came to the North Bay—there was no freedom. The following are those known to have been enslaved when they arrived in the San Francisco North Bay:

Napa County

On January 15, 1846, thirty five men, women, and children were sold in St. Helena in Napa County. For more than $9,500, John B. and Mary E. Scott sold the enslaved men, women, and children to Charles S. Carrington and John S. Field.[49] They included:

Moses and Judy and their seven children:
Judy, Kiker, Tyree, Tom, Penelope, Moses, and Martha

Steven and Rebecca and her three children:
Nat, Lewis, and Ira

---

49   A Deed For Sale of Slaves, Napa Historical Society.

William and Eliza and child:
Ephraim

Robin and Sophia and her three children:
Washington, Peggy, and Patsey

Leitha and her child:
Minerva

Mildred and her child:
Nancy

Charity and her two children:
Martha and Elizabeth

Thomas
Catherine
Harriet
Steve
Booker
Cupid

Other men and women known to be enslaved in Napa were:

Esther Seawell (who later married Joseph S. Hatton)
Abraham Seawell
Matilda Seawell
Old Man Sours
Old Man Syde
Aaron Rice
Wash Strain

Solano County:

An index of the 1850 census noted that fourteen enslaved men
and one woman were in Solano County working under "contract"
for two years. They were:

From Missouri:

Bill, 20
Hirds, 24
Isaac, 30
Peter, 18
Thomas, 22

From Kentucky:

Bolin, 26
Higgins, 21
Joe, 27
Jim, 30
Cowins, 27
Joe, 28
Minerva, 40
Graciel, 34
Whitehead, 27

Other Solano County men and women known to be enslaved were:
John Grider
Nancy Geary
Catherine Jackson
Adam Willis

Sonoma County

Jacob Graham

Delegates to the 1857 Colored Citizens Convention reported that twenty-six men were being held as slaves on remote farms in the county.[50]

---

50 Lapp, Rudolph M. *Blacks in Gold Rush Country*, Yale University Press, 1995.

Appendix G: Early Vallejo Map

John Grider was a familiar sight along the streets of
Vallejo in the mid 1800s to early 1900s. Courtesy of
the Vallejo Naval and Historical Museum.

1. Vallejo's first public school. Now the location of Lincoln
   Elementary School at Sonoma Boulevard and Carolina
   Street.

2. Methodist Episcopal Church. Founded by David Farragut, the first commandant of Mare Island, this church sold its sanctuary to Kyles Temple AME Zion Church in 1919.
3. Brownlie's Livery Stable. John Grider worked at the livery stable for many years.
4. Mike Dervin's Butcher Shop. Grider worked for Derwin for a number of years.
5. After a long work day Grider would clean his horses by swimming them in the bay from the Capitol Street to York Street wharves.
6. The United States Hotel at the foot of Maine Street was the location of Vallejo's colored school in the late 1850s and 1860sl.
7. Vallejo's Capitol Building. It's here where the California Fugitive Slave Act was passed into law.
8. The Central Hotel (also known as Wyatt's Hotel) was owned by George H. Wyatt. Grider was enslaved to Wyatt when he arrived in California in the 1840s.

Recommended Research Resources

When I started researching this history, I had no outline and only a vague notion of what I wanted to find out about Vallejo African Americans in the 1800s. Except for John Grider's name, I had no solid dates in mind. I soon learned that while curiosity can get you started in researching historic data, that curiosity can and will fade if you are too vague about what you want to research. A general idea about a person, place, or thing is a must to get you started on researching a historic subject.

I did know John Grider's name and that he lived in Vallejo in the 1800s and early 1900s, but I really had no clue as to where to find information on him. With some exceptions, the nineteenth century "white" press generally ignored black people and their contributions. Obituaries were usually the exception, especially if a black man or woman had been a longtime resident of the community and was generally liked by whites. Grider, for example was praised with a front obituary in December 1924, but he was ignored for the majority of his ninety-eight years. Regional historians who compiled *The History of Solano, The History of Solano and Napa Counties, The History of Napa and Lake Counties,* and *The History of Sonoma County* made scant mention of black people and, even then, no names were mentioned.

I soon learned to focus my research after spending a frustrating afternoon looking through nineteenth century Vallejo newspapers at my local library and coming up with absolutely nothing. Fortunately, I remembered some advice I received from Guy Washington, who had reminded me to search several places, including old city directories. At the library, I found a well-worn 1869 Vallejo city directory. I turned to the "G" listing and there was "Grider, Jno." He worked as a hostler (someone who works with horses) at a Virginia Street livery stable then owned by George Higson. I caught my breath. I read the line again. From that point on John Grider became real.

With the discovery of Grider's name in that and several other directories—in an 1870 directory he is listed as working for the Brownlie livery station at 134 Virginia Street—I expanded my search for other African Americans living in the North Bay in the 1800s. Fortunately, the African American press wrote about the nineteenth century North Bay black community extensively. I've learned a great deal more about African Americans in Solano, Napa, and Sonoma counties as a result of looking in a variety of places.

These are some of the valuable resources I turned to throughout my research.

African American Genealogical Society of Northern California
PO Box 10942
Oakland, CA 94610
www.Aagsnc.org

African American Museum and Library at Oakland
659 14th St.
Oakland, CA 94612
(510) 637-0200

www.Ancestry.com

Bancroft Library, U.C. Berkeley
University of California
Berkeley, CA 94720-6000
(510) 642-6481

Benicia Historical Society
132 West E Street
Benicia, CA 94510-3172
(707) 745-1822

Berkshire County Historical Society
780 Holmes Road
Pittsfield, MA 01201
413) 442-1793

Calaveras County Historical Society
PO Box 721
30 N. Main St.
San Andreas, CA 95249
(209) 754-1058

The California Digital Newspaper Collection: cdnc.ucr.edu/

This project offers over 200,000 pages of California newspapers
spanning the years 1849-1911: the *Alta California,* 1849-1891; the
San Francisco Call, 1893-1910; *the Amador Ledger,* 1900-1911; *the
Imperial Valley Press,* 1901-1911; the *Sacramento Record-Union,*
1859-1890; and the *Los Angeles Herald,* 1905-1907. At this site
I found a number of obituaries of early black pioneers who, by
the early 1900s, were starting to die off. *The San Francisco Call*
provides numerous articles on Buffalo Soldiers who were stationed
at the Presidio in the late 1800s and early 1900s.

California Historical Society
678 Mission Street

San Francisco, CA 94109
(415) 357-1848

California Underground Railroad Digital Archives
(916) 278-3510
California State University, Sacramento
digital.lib.csus.edu/curr/curr.team.html

Technology has served me well in documenting the African American presence in our region. Digitized copies of *The Elevator* 1865 to 1871 can be found on the California Underground Railroad Digital Archives website.

The entire collection of *The Elevator* (1865–1898) as well as other early black newspapers, including *The Mirror of the Times* (1855–1857) and *The Pacific Appeal* (1862–1880), can be found on microfilm at some county libraries in Oakland, San Francisco, and Sacramento. Many of these newspapers are at area colleges and universities. For anyone researching early Bay Area black history these newspapers are essential. These early black newspapers relied on agents, who would collect subscriptions and share news from their respective communities. These newspapers detailed blacks' struggles for equal rights both statewide and locally in the North Bay communities of Vallejo, Benicia, Suisun, Napa, Santa Rosa, and Petaluma.

Dixon Public Library
230 N. 1st Street
Dixon, CA 95620
(707) 678-5447

John F. Kennedy Library
505 Santa Clara Street
Vallejo, CA 94590
(866) 553-5568

The Library of Congress
101 Independence Ave., SE
Washington, DC 20540
(202) 707-4700
The mission of the National Digital Newspaper Program, under the auspices of the Library of Congress (LOC), is to digitize thousands of newspapers from all over the United States and its territories. While the complete digitization process will take many years, the LOC has already digitized a small nationwide sampling of newspapers from 1900 to 1910.

Mare Island Museum
Railroad Avenue and 8th Street
Mare Island, CA 94590
(707) 557-1538

Most Worshipful Prince Hall Grand Lodge
State of California, Inc.
9027 South Figuero St.
Los Angeles, CA 90003
(323) 242-2393

The Grand Lodge had digitized its proceedings dating back to 1855. These amazing records are available on compact discs and can be ordered from the address above.

Museum of the African Diaspora, San Francisco
685 Mission Street San Francisco, CA 94105
(415) 3580-7200

Napa County Historical Society
1219 1st St
Napa, CA 4559
(707) 224-1739

The National Archives and Records Administration
8601 Adelphi Road
College Park, MD 20740-6001
(866) 272-6272

National Park Service, Pacific West Regional
The National Underground Network to Freedom
1111 Jackson Street, Suite 700
Oakland, CA 94607
(510) 561- 4485 / (510) 817-1390

I heard about this program through a friend, Morris Turner, who had written a book about black towns and settlements. It was through Morris that I met Guy Washington, regional director of the Underground Railroad Network to Freedom Project for this region.

NewspaperArchive.com
This is a great site. While the website charges a nominal monthly fee, I got my money's worth in the first couple of weeks of research on the site. Primarily I used the site, which has newspapers dating from 1759 through the present day, to research the *Oakland Tribune*, which covered Vallejo and the North Bay extensively during the early 1900s. I found several articles dealing with the 1919 Kyles Temple AME Church fire in Vallejo as well as the subsequent trial of the man accused of setting the fire. I also found Delilah L. Beasley's columns and her obituary at this site.

The Elevator, a San Francisco-based black newspaper
published from 1856 to 1898, covered events and residents
of the North Bay in the nineteenth century.

Petaluma Historical Library and Museum
20 Fourth Street
Petaluma, CA 94952
(707) 778-4398

Santa Rosa Rural Cemetery
Contact: Santa Rosa Recreation & Parks Department
(707) 543-3292

Slavery Era Insurance Registry
California Department of Insurance
www.insurance.ca.gov/0100-consumers/0300-public-programs/0200-slavery-era-insur

Solano County Archives
815 Chadbourne Rd, Suite 120
Fairfield, CA 94534
(707) 434-1101
Old documents such as property deeds, voter rolls, the 1863 Union draft, and census records are housed at the Solano County Archives.
Solano County Genealogical Society
Sonoma County Historical Society
P.O. Box 3009
Fairfield, CA 94533

Solano County Library
solanolibrary.com

Vacaville Heritage Council
610 E. Main Street
Vacaville, CA 95688
(707) 447-0518

Vacaville Museum

213 Buck Ave
Vacaville, CA 95688
(707) 447-4513

Vallejo Naval and Historical Museum
734 Marin Street
Vallejo, CA 94590
(707) 643-0077
Historic documents, photographs, newspapers, artifacts, and city directories are housed here. Jim Kern, museum director, showed me the photo of the Vallejo Society of California Pioneers, in which John Grider stood as the lone African American of the group.

For more information and resources, visit North Bay Black Roots online at www.northbayblackroots.com.

References

Delilah L. Beasley: The Memory-Keeper

Beasley, Delilah L. *The Negro Trail Blazers of California* Negro University Press (1969)

Crouchett, Lorraine J. *Delilah Leontium Beasley Oakland's Crusading Journalist Downy Place Publishing House, Inc. (1990)*

Pittman, Tarea Hall. *NAACP Official and Civil Rights Worker*, 1971-1972, typescript of an oral history conducted 1971-1972 by Joyce Henderson, Regional Oral History Office, The Bancroft Library, University of California, Berkeley, page 82.

John Grider's Century: A Black Bear Flag Veteran

Beasley, Delilah L. *The Negro Trail Blazers of California*, p. 125

Bowman, Alan P. *Index to the 1850 Census of the State of California.* Genealogical Publishing Co., Inc. Baltimore (1972)

City, county directories from 1869, 1870, 1871, 1874, 1879 and 1896.

Coke Wood, Richard. (1949) *Murphy's, Queen of the Sierra, p.5.* Published by the *Calaveras Californian.*

Dutton, David. et al. *The History of Solano County. Wood Alley and Co., San Francisco (1879)*

Elevator, The

The History of Napa and Lake Counties

Hook, J. W. Bishop. *The Hundred Years of the African Methodist Episcopal Zion Church, or the Centennial of African Methodism (1895)*

Moore, Jamison, John Bishop. *The History of The AME Zion Church in America (1884)*

Napa County Register

Napa Daily Register

Napa Reporter, The

Modesto Bee, The

Noyes, Leonard Withington. *Diary of Leonard Withington Noyes* (1850-1868)), p. 46.

Pacific Appeal, The

Parish, John C. *A Project For A California Slave Colony. The Huntington Library Bulletin (1935*

Petaluma Argus

Santa Rosa Times, The

Slaves in Napa County: A Deed For Sale of Slaves. January 15, 1846. St. Helena

Solano deed and probate records, Solano County Archives

Vallejo Evening Chronicle, The

Vallejo Times Herald, September 11, 1914. "Previous Celebrations Are Eclipsed By Splendid Pageant Given By Vallejo.

Webster, Calvin B. *Educational History of Solano County. Bancroft Co., San Francisco (1889)*

New Beginnings

Vallejo City Directory

Solano County Directory

Black Abolitionists Archives, University of Detroit

The Elevator

Solano County Great Register

The Vallejo Evening Chronicle

Leading the Way

Proceedings of the California Conventions of Colored Citizens, 1855, 1856 and 1865

1860, 1870 U.S. Census

The Elevator

History of the Most Worshipful Prince Hall Grand Lodge State of California, Inc., 150th Anniversary Year Book

Proceedings, Prince Hall Masons California Grand Lodge from 1855–1900

Prince Hall Masonic Digest, Official Publication of the Prince Hall Grand Lodge of Free and Accepted Masons of California and Jurisdictions Inc., Vol. 16, June 1971. Pg. 30.

We Were Here: Profiles of North Bay African Americans in the Nineteenth Century

Adam Willis

Property deeds, Solano County Archive

The Elevator

U.S. Census 1860, 1870, 1880 and 1900

The Landeways

J. R. Landeway letter, Elizabeth (Landeway) Venable. September 4, 1930. California Historical Society

The Elevator

1860, 1870, 1880 Census

San Francisco Call (1885)

Probate records of George and Elizabeth Van Blake March 23, 1918

George and Elizabeth Van Blake

Beasley, Delilah L. *The Negro Trail Blazers of California*

The Vallejo Evening Chronicle

The Vallejo City Directory

Probate Records, Solano County Archives

Grafton T. Brown

Sketch of Santa Rosa Academy by Grafton T. Brown, Bancroft
   Library, U.C. Berkeley, The Robert H. Honeyman Collection
Reps, John W., *Views and Viewmakers of Urban America: Lithographs
   of Towns and Cities in The United States and Canada, Notes On
   The Artists and Publishers, and A Union Catalog of Their Work,
   1825–1925* (University of Missouri Press, 1985).
Photo of Grafton T. Brown, California Historical Society

New Century Brings New Hopes and New Concerns for North Bay black Residents

The Vallejo Evening Chronicle
The San Francisco Call
The Oakland Tribune
The Papers of the National Association for the Advancement of
   Colored People, Vallejo branch, Library of Congress
History of the Most Worshipful Prince Hall Grand Lodge State
   of California, Inc., 150th Anniversary Year Book
Proceedings, Prince Hall Masons California Grand Lodge from
   1855–1900
Amerson, A. Wayne, *Northern California and its Challenges to a
   Negro in the mid-1900s,* typescript of an oral history conducted
   1972 by Joyce Henderson, Regional Oral History Office, The
   Bancroft Library, University of California, Berkeley, page 103.
   The Earl Warren Oral History Project.

A. Wayne Amerson: The Twentieth-Century Memory Keeper

Amerson, A. Wayne, *Northern California and its Challenges to a
   Negro in the mid-1900s,* typescript of an oral history conducted
   1972 by Joyce Henderson, Regional Oral History Office, The
   Bancroft Library, University of California, Berkeley, page 103.
   The Earl Warren Oral History Project.

Other Early Families

Beasley, Delilah L. *The Negro Trail Blazers of California*

Sonoma County History and Genealogy Library
The Elevator
The Pacific Appeal

Gravestones Mark the Final Resting Place of Many Early North Bay African Americans

A compilation of notes from Solano County Archives, Benicia Historical Society, and the Sonoma County Library History and Genealogy Library.

Students Enrolled in the Vallejo Industrial and Normal School, 1916

Article compiled from a newspaper article among the papers of A. Wayne Amerson, stored at the Bancroft Library, U.C. Berkeley.

Prince Hall Masons, Firma Lodge No. 27, Vallejo Membership List, 1918

Firma Lodge No. 27, book of minutes, 1918–1925

NAACP Vallejo Branch Original Membership List, 1917

The Records of the National Association for the Advancement of Colored People, Vallejo branch, Library of Congress

Slavery in the North Bay

Deed of Trust, John B. and Mary E. Scott, January 15, 1846
The Napa Register
Beasley, Delilah L. *The Negro Trail Blazers of California*
Bowman, Alan P. *Index to the 1850 Census of the State of California,* 1972
Lapp, Rudolph M. *Blacks in Gold Rush California,* Yale University Press, 1995

Early Vallejo Map

Illustration, George Manyik, 1943

Index

Anderson, Ivy xvi, 81, 82
Appomattox Court House
    xxiii
Atkinson, E. C. 73

B

Bailey, William 32
Baker, Squire xvi, 42, 99, 100
Bancroft Library 56, 57, 83,
    134, 140, 143, 144
barbers xv, 35, 38
Battleship *Maine* xxiv
Beach, Commandant E. L. 69
Bear Flag vii, xii, xv, xviii, xxi,
    xxiv, xxvi, 3, 7, 8, 9, 10,
    11, 18, 19, 40, 55, 86,
    97, 115, 140
Bear Flag Republic 8
Bear Flag Revolt vii, xii, xviii,
    xxi, xxvi, 3, 8, 10, 11
Bear Flag veteran xxiv, 11, 19,
    55, 86, 115
Beasley, Delilah L. *The Negro
    Trail Blazers of Califor-
    nia* xi
"Ben" 9
Benicia City Cemetery 110
Benicia courtroom 15, 50
Bethel AME Church xxiv
Billy Gaston 9
black clerks xiii, 62
Blue Rock Springs 14
Bodega 109
Bradford, Rebecca 88
Brannan Guard 98

Breck, Rev. J. Lloyd 94
Briscoe, Erastus 35, 98
British Columbia 17, 18, 57
Brother Jonathan 18
Brown, Grafton T. viii, xvi, 56,
    57, 142, 143
Brown, John xxiii, xxiv, 42,
    116
Brownlie, John 12, 13
Brownlie's Livery Stable 131
Brown, Pink 42
Brunson, Lewis 101
Buffalo Soldiers xiii, xv, 44,
    46, 59, 134
Bundy, Dr. LeRoy 68
Bundy, Elizabeth xxiii, 84,
    94, 110
Burney, James 11

C

Calaveras Californian 140
Calaveras County 12, 15, 134
California Assembly 15
California Federation of Col-
    ored Women's Clubs 4
California Fugitive Slave Act
    131
California Relief Administra-
    tion 84
California statehood xviii, 9
Canada 18, 94, 143
Canner, Paul 88
Cape Horn 53
Capitol Building 131
Capitol Hotel 13

Captain Charles Young Camp
6, Department of the
Columbia, United Span-
ish War Veterans. 45
Carquinez Cemetery 111
Carquinez Hotel 30, 102
Cason, J. H. 30, 94, 99
Caviel, A. B. 55, 62, 121,
125
C.C. Courtney 34
Central Hotel 131
Charles Courtney 59
Christopher, William 31
Churchman, William 24
Civil War vii, xxii, xxiii, 34,
35, 38, 103, 111
Clanton, S. P. 35, 38, 95
Clark, John Balfour 42, 101
Clay, Kentucky 94
Clear Lake 90, 92
Clopton, F. D. 68, 124, 125
Cloverdale 109
Colfax Guard 105
colored school xxiv, 22, 23,
74, 104, 131
Connolly, Henry 14
Convention of the Colored
Citizens of the State of
California xxii, xxiii
Corbin, D. G. 34, 68, 70
Cornell Baptist Church 65
Crabb, Henry A. 15
Crooks, Robert xxiv, 105
Crouchett, Lorraine J. 5, 140
Curtee, Edward 42

Cyanne 91
Cypress Hill Cemetery 111,
112

D

Delilah L. Beasley Club 5
*Delilah Leontium Beasley: Oak-
land's Crusading Journal-
ist* 5
Dennis, Rev. J. A. 65
Derrick, F.W. 13
Dervin, Mike 13, 131
Dinwiddie County, Virginia
94
Dixon, Wilson 30, 54, 102
Dodson, Jacob 9
Dolores Owens Cofer xii, 60
Donner Party xxiv, 105
Dr. Rodgers 33
Duff, James 9, 10

E

Early Entrepreneurs vii, 28
East St. Louis, Illinois 68
Edwards, Rev. S. E. 71
El Dorado xxv, 39
Ellsworth Courtney xv, xxv,
27
Emancipation Day 36
Emancipation Proclamation
xxii, xxiii, 35, 95, 98
Eugene C. Berry 62

F